Walt Buescher's Library of Humor

Walt Buescher's Library of Humor

Walter M. Buescher

Prentice-Hall, Inc.
Englewood Cliffs, New Jersey

Prentice-Hall International, Inc., *London*
Prentice-Hall of Australia, Pty. Ltd., *Sydney*
Prentice-Hall Canada, Inc., *Toronto*
Prentice-Hall of India Private Ltd., *New Delhi*
Prentice-Hall of Japan, Inc., *Tokyo*
Prentice-Hall of Southeast Asia Pte. Ltd., *Singapore*
Whitehall Books, Ltd., *Wellington, New Zealand*
Editora Prentice-Hall do Brasil, Ltda., *Rio de Janeiro*

Library of Congress Cataloging in Publication Data
Buescher, Walter M.
   Walt Buescher's I ibrary of humor.

   Includes index.
   1. Public speaking—Handbooks, manuals, etc.
2. American wit and humor. I. Title. II. Title: Library
of humor.
PN4193.15B8   1984   818'.5402   83-24656

ISBN 0-13-944199-9 {PBK}

ISBN 0-13-944207-3

Printed in the United States of America

A cheerful heart is good medicine.

Proverbs 17:22

To my good wife Norma, who has listened to me tell these stories at meetings and conventions a thousand times, but who still laughs as if she is hearing them for the first time.

Foreword

If all the lackluster convention speakers, tedious sales-meeting speakers, boring script writers, and dispirited MCs were laid end-to-end, what a boon to mankind that would be!

The very fact that you are holding this book in your hands is proof that you are determined not to join that undistinguished sorority or fraternity.

How often have we agonized while some "authority in his field— a man who needs no introduction" droned on and on, providing sleep to people afflicted with chronic and congenital sleeplessness— people who have given up on Sominex and whose malady has been abandoned as hopeless by the medical profession? Today, accommodating hotel managers provide convention rooms that sleep up to five hundred people.

You know that all this tedium is unnecessary and so do we. Speakers, MCs and script writers can be *interesting*! This book is your insurance policy against uninteresting speeches and scripts. Whether you are a politician seeking reelection, a druggist addressing a trade association convention, or an engineer speaking at a service club meeting, *your presentation can be outstanding*!

How do you prepare for a speech or script? Chances are that you do just as we do. First the serious portion of the speech or script is outlined in logical sequence. Then the speech or script is punctuated with humor. You know that humor is the best antidote for a flat speech or script. The Creator gave animals five senses, but he gave man six. The sixth is the sense of humor. That sixth sense sets man apart. We speakers and script writers capitalize on that fact.

We know that *humor makes people feel good*! People who feel good get things done! Achievers are seldom sad, angry, or disgusted. People who feel good have a "Can-Do" attitude. That's the attitude that you want to transmit to your audience!

Who invented recess? Almost surely it was a teacher who found that students learn more with recess than without. Because we have experienced it in ourselves, we know that the human mind takes periodic mental recesses. It happens to the Ph.D. as often as it happens to the illiterate. That is why we slip illustrative humorous

vii

stories or one-liners into our speeches and scripts. When the human mind is about to take a recess, *we give it a recess with humor*.

We *use humor as a memory hook*. Memory experts teach memory through association. For instance, we know that these will be forgotten: Our Model SX-7 is fast. The evidence is confusing. He was gone for a long time. It is impossible. But these will be remembered: Our Model SX-7 is faster than a nudist who has spilled coffee in his lap. When you hear and read all this, you'll be so confused that you won't know whether you have found a rope or lost a mule. He was gone longer than the gestation period of an elephant. It is as impossible as making birth control retroactive.

We use humor because we know it adds credibility. People at a convention will accept as gospel truth the words of an interesting speaker, while they harbor doubts about the words of a wearisome speaker. "Our Model SX-7 is fast," will prompt skeptical reactions. "How fast?" "That's what they all say." "I'll bet the competition is faster." However when we use our previously mentioned memory hook, "Our Model SX-7 is faster than a nudist who has spilled coffee in his lap," there will be no doubt about the speed of the SX-7. Instead the audience will smile and wonder just how fast that nudist zoomed out of there.

We script writers and speakers know that humor disarms. Will Rogers was a master of the art. To the joy or dismay of partisans, his quote, "Prohibition is better than no liquor at all," did more to bring Repeal than any one-hour speech on the floor of Congress or any 50-page study could have done.

We hope that you get the same enthusiastic response from the stories in this book that we have gotten in thirty years of speech and script preparation. We have platform-tested most of the entries in this book. We would have no hesitation to use the rest.

Finally, here is one of those multiple-choice tests that are so popular in newspapers and magazines nowadays. . . .

Please check one:

☐ 1. I want more standing ovations with thunderous applause.
☐ 2. I will be satisfied with sitting ovations with scant sign of audience approval.

If you checked #1, please read on.

Walter M. Buescher

Preface

Every good speaker and script writer knows that a humorous story must be appropriate. It must fit! To be sure that you find material that will fit, we have provided four ways to identify just the right story for your presentation.

1. *Topical headings.* Key words are alphabetized in 398 headings. Your search begins here!

2. *Numbers under stories.* You will note that the stories are numbered consecutively from one to 1,421. Under many stories you will find other numbers. These are entries that fit another chapter heading best, but they still have pertinence to the chapter headings under which they are found. One of these may be just what you are looking for!

3. *Phrase cross-reference.* Suppose you have the sentence, "Who said it would be easy?" in your presentation, and you want to illustrate that sentence with a memory hook. In the phrase cross-reference, you will find, "Easy?, Who said it would be—197, 316, 317, etc." Look up these story numbers to see which one best illustrates what you wish to say.

The phrases are alphabetized by the key word in each phrase. We believe you will find this unusual cross-reference feature one of the most helpful in the whole book.

4. *Word cross-reference.* Suppose you wish to say something amusing about your husband. In the word cross-reference you will find, "Husband—131, 294, 354, 385, 396," and so on. Surely in that assortment of story numbers you will find something that will make you sound like Erma Bombeck.

We also call attention to four parts of this book that will prove helpful to you in special cases:

1. *MC.* If you are appointed Master/Mistress of Ceremonies, here is a chapter heading that will give you a wealth of material to draw from.

2. *Need some one-liners?* You will find a good assortment of one-sentence humor in the Axioms and Philosophy sections of the book. Ditch those tired old platitudes and substitute some lively, platform-tested one-liners from these two chapters.

3. *Platform emergencies.* What happens if your story produces nothing but deafening silence? What happens if the mike goes dead? Platform emergencies will help you hurdle the occupational hazards of our profession.

4. *Public speaking.* Under this chapter heading you will find response to introductions and a wide assortment of material that can be used in your speech or script. This potpourri can help you get your presentation off to a rousing start!

Like a bikini at the beach, the stories in this volume cover the bare essentials. A minimum number of words are used to get to the punch line. By cutting nonessential verbiage, we are able to give you a much larger selection of humorous material.

You will have no difficulty adding flesh to the bare bones that we have provided. You will have no problem updating some stories, adding local color to others. You know from experience that this makes the story go over better.

Best wishes for a standing ovation after your presentation!

Walt Buescher

Acknowledgment

The author hereby expresses his sincere appreciation to all those hosts of long-forgotten persons from whom the stories in the book were "borrowed" in thirty years on the public platform. The author knows that these anonymous contributors are equally thankful to the forgotten persons from whom they "borrowed" the stories in this Library.

The author makes no claim of originality for most of the entries in the Library, even though constant use and re-use has sometimes given the author illusions of originality. The author accepts responsibility for the manner in which the stories were edited into skeleton form so that more humorous material would be available to the reader. It is hoped that the user of this Library of Humor will likewise borrow, edit, remodel, localize, up-date and otherwise adapt the material to suit his or her own purposes, needs and personality.

W.M.B.

Contents

X

Z

A

Accident

1. My wife called to say that the car was flooded. It sure was. She had driven it into the St. Joe River.

2. He called a spade a spade until he stumbled over one in the dark and then he called it a . . .

3. A girl who ordinarily complained about heavy traffic went out on Sunday morning. She thought there would be nobody around. She thought the Catholics would be at Mass and the Protestants would be in bed. But she was run down by a Seventh Day Adventist.

4. My wife backed the car out of the garage. In itself, that isn't bad, but I had backed the car into the garage.

69, 90, 304, 445, 636, 1074, 1157, 1199, 1240

Accounts Receivable

5. If you don't pay your bill by next Saturday, we will tell the rest of your creditors you did.

6. Business is improving. I can tell. People are beginning to take their bills out of the envelopes again.

7. I would have worn my mink stole to the party our auto dealer was throwing, but then he might have insisted that I pay our past-due repair bills.

8. "We have your order but will not ship it until you pay for the last three orders we shipped you."
   "I can't wait that long. Cancel the order."

157, 399, 400, 405, 724, 847, 913, 1137

1

Achievement

9. "It's wonderful what some insects can do. A grasshopper can jump 200 times its own length."

"That's nothing. I saw a tiny wasp raise a 200-pound man three feet off the ground."

10. He came to class five minutes early every day. In more ways than one, he was in a class by himself.

11. Three ways to achieve:
    1. Do it yourself.
    2. Hire someone to do it.
    3. Forbid your kids to do it.

Activists

12. The truth has surfaced about the case of Little Red Riding Hood. When the wolf was tried in circuit court, the judge dismissed the case because the wolf had not been informed of his rights. The ACLU provided an attorney for the wolf and the attorney entered a self-defense plea. The ACLU barrister said the wolf was only "doing his thing."

After the wolf was released, Little Red Riding Hood, her grand-mother, and the woodchopper were arrested on charges of assault and battery with a deadly weapon. The three miscreants are now in prison, and properly so. Grandma's house has been turned into a national shrine. On dedication day, the nation's foremost activists were there. When Jane Fonda spoke about the human-rights violations against the wolf, there wasn't a dry eye in the house.

Adolescence

13. Adolescence is when a boy graduates from a Mickey Mouse watch to a copy of *Playboy* hidden under the mattress.

Advertising

14. One of the auto companies had a fat, cigar-smoking sheriff in one of their commercials. The Wisconsin Sheriffs' Association objected because they said the ads ridiculed their people. All of us who have felt right along that people in government have no sense of humor now have it confirmed from Wisconsin.

15. If you are in business and do not advertise, it is like winking at a pretty girl in the dark. You know *you* are interested, but does *she* know?

16. Want ad: Swimming pool for sale. Owned by a little old lady who only swam in it once.

17. Sign on music truck: Drive Carefully. We're Out of Harps.

91, 143, 250, 647, 762, 1009, 1057, 1169, 1337

Affirmative Action

18. "Your name is Johann Frederick Schultz and you want to change it to Fernando Roberto Lopez. Why?"
    "So I can get a job."

Air Transport

19. Headline: Jet Sets Speed Record of 822 MPH.
    That beats the previous speed record set by Joe Franklin, who, in a parking lot in Knoxville, backed a car going 739 mph into a parking space four inches wider than the auto he was driving.

20. A sure way to catch a plane is to miss the one before.

21. A pilot on a rough flight didn't ease our feelings any when he came through the cabin carrying a book entitled, *How to Fly in Twenty Easy Lessons.*

22. One new flight attendant, subjected to the usual hazing that new attendants get, had a father who was a pharmacist. Her Dad gave her some drops to put into the pilots' coffee. The pilots and medical science are still baffled about the malady the pilots contracted.

23. Marine pilots come in with a wheels-up landing every so often. It doesn't bother them. It just takes a little more power to get to the ramp.

24. An airline pilot, miffed because he had been placed on a freight run, took the names off of the coffins he carried. He then obtained some of those "tell-us-how-you-liked-our-service" forms, filled them out in the corpses' names, and sent them to the vice president of the airline. He wrote that the service was lousy and he would never fly on that airline again.
    The airline frantically struggled to find the writers of these letters and eventually found them six feet under. Then the vice president's intuition told him who had written the letters. The pilot suggested a compromise. He's back on a people run instead of a freight run.

25. The pilot came in with a wheels-up landing.
    The tower called, "May we be of assistance?"
    "I'm sure glad you asked that question," said the pilot.

26. The navigator was lost. "I don't know where we are, but we're sure making good time," he said.

27. Flying: Hours of boredom mixed with moments of terror.

28. When a flight attendant for a West Coast airline was asked what "Grand Tetons" meant in English, she blushed and said, "Sweater Girl Mountains."

29. The PA came on. "You are flying on the new Model XL-300, a marvel in aeronautical engineering. There is no pilot in the pilot's compartment. Everything is being operated from the ground. We took off from Los Angeles by computer. We are followed by tracking stations across the country. We will land in New York by computer. You need have no fear, however, because nothing can go wrong, can go wrong, can go wrong, can go wrong, can go wrong, can go wrong."

30. God must have loved airline fares. He gave us so many of them.

31. "Don't be afraid to fly. The Bible says, 'I will be with you always.'"

    "Read that passage again. It says, 'Lo, l-o-w, I will be with you always.' "

32. "Those of you sitting on the left side of the plane have probably observed by now that one of the engines is not running. Do not worry. It will delay us only about twenty minutes."

    "Those of you sitting on the right side of the plane have probably observed by now that one of the engines is not running there either. However, do not worry. This plane can fly with two engines. We will be about forty minutes late in our arrival."

    "Those of you sitting on the left side of the plane have probably observed at this point that neither engine is running there. Do not fear. We can fly with one engine, but we will be an hour and fifteen minutes late on arrival."

    Said a passenger to his seat-mate: "I sure hope that fourth engine doesn't go out. We could be up here all night."

33. When miniskirts gave way to skirts below the knee, United Airlines went along with the fashion. No longer do we see the friendly thighs of United.

34. The Dallas-Fort Worth Airport is so big that the people who work on the north side of the terminal wear blue and those on the south side wear gray.

35. Two caterpillars eyeballing a butterfly overhead:

    "You'd never get me up in one of those things for a million bucks."

36. Flier to tower: "One engine is dead. Gasoline is leaking. One of my wing flaps is broken. My oil pressure is near zero. What should I do?"

Tower to flier: "Repeat after me, 'Our Father who art in Heaven, hallowed be thy name . . .' "

429, 556

Animal

37. A ram ran over the cliff. He didn't see the ewe turn.

38. Show me a home where the buffalo roam and I'll show you a pretty smelly living room.

39. "When I was in Africa, a lion ran across my path. I had no gun, so I threw a pail of water at him and he ran away."
   "I'll vouch for that. When I petted the lion's mane, it was still wet."

40. Two rats were eating their way through a bag of grain.
   "What a way to make a living!"
   "Agreed, but it sure beats those environmentalist laboratories."

41. Boy ostriches were chasing the girl ostriches. The girl ostriches hid their heads in the sand. One boy ostrich said to another, "I wonder where the girls went."

42. In Washington, they ban everything at the drop of a rat.

43. "This snake snapped at me."
   "Snakes don't snap."
   "This one did. It's a garter snake."

See Cat, Dog, Cow, etc.

Antique

44. The quickest way to get kicked out of an antique shop is to go in and ask, "What's new?"

124

Antisocial

45. Do you growl inside when the head waitress shunts you into the bar before seating you? Are you less than cheerful when someone calls at 2:30 a.m. and it's a wrong number? Do you think seventeen people in a van are too many? Do you think 150 people in a small room are too many at a cocktail party? Do you feel chauvinistic when you try to get out of an elevator and there are six women blocking your way? Are you irritable and restless when you have to stand in line at the airport for twenty-seven minutes? Do you churn inside when the woman at the search-and-seizure stall at the airport makes

you take off your pants because your zipper is triggering her anti-hijack gizmo?

Is that the way you feel? I've got news for you. You're antisocial.

Appearance

46. Her hair looks like an explosion in a mattress factory.

47. He looked like a sack of cats going to the river.

Army

48. "You didn't salute. How long have you been in the Army?"
"All day, sir."

49. "We've got a case of beriberi here."
"Send it to the Marines. They'll drink anything."

50. "Are you interested in a commission?"
"No, I'd rather just take straight salary."

51. General at press conference: "Remember, gentlemen, that the enemy has generals, too. And they make mistakes, too."

52. Sign on a military road: Drive carefully. Don't hit your replacement.

53. I'm sorry I'm late, folks, but my old commanding officer left me off at the wrong floor.

54. British officer in Rangoon: "I can understand your eye-openers in the morning, your flavoring of morning tea. I can understand a drink before lunch and flavoring your afternoon tea. I can understand cocktails before dinner and an after-dinner drink. I can understand a nightcap before retiring, but this nipping in between has got to stop."

55. A steno who wasn't used to Army lingo typed "intelligent officer" instead of "Intelligence Officer."

"My dear young lady, who ever heard of an intelligent officer?"

56. "Watson here. Brigadier general. Married. Two sons. One a doctor. One at West Point."

"Johnson here. Brigadier general. Married. Two sons. Both in space administration."

"Wilkins here. Sergeant. Unmarried. Two sons. Both Brigadier generals."

57. The Army has a new missile called Civil Service. They can't get it to work and can't fire it.

58. Officers and noncoms were at rest camp. The Commanding officer suggested a game of soccer, but explained, "In soccer, you kick the ball, but sometimes you accidentally kick each other."

Major: "Let's play. Where's the ball?"
Private: "Who needs a ball? Let's get going."

59. The recruit was told to challenge anyone at the gate who didn't have a blue card.

General Jenkins came through. He didn't have his blue card with him. The recruit challenged the general. The general said he was coming in anyway.

Private: "Who do I shoot? You or the driver? I'm new at this guard-duty business."

60. "Fancy that," said the proud mother. "They've promoted our Herbert for hittin' his sergeant. They've made him a court martial."

572, 766, 945, 1127, 1166, 1354, 1355, 1370

Art and Artists

61. Al Capp on the subject of abstract art: "A product of the untalented, sold by the unprincipled to the utterly bewildered."

62. Mark Twain on the subject of modern art: "It looks like a tortoise-shell cat having a fit in a platter of tomatoes."

63. Matisse's *Le Bateau* hung upside-down in a New York art museum for a whole year without anyone's noticing.

It's still a mystery how anyone could tell which was right-side-up.

64. Picasso was robbed. He gave the police a drawing of the robber. In short order, the Paris police caught a suspect. He was a one-eyed ballet dancer carrying a limp Eiffel Tower over his right shoulder and a wheelbarrow under his left arm.

Attention

65. If you hear the words, "two-by-four principle," the speaker is referring to this classic story:

An Arkansas farmer told his hired man to treat his mule gently. When the mule wouldn't move, the farmer picked up a two-by-four and clubbed the mule over the rump.

"But I thought you told me to treat him gently."

"That's right. But you've got to get his attention first."

702, 1083

Attorney

66. "You're a crook."
"You're a liar."

Judge: "Now that the opposing attorneys have been properly introduced, let us start this case."

67. Doctor: "While I don't say that all lawyers are crooks, you'll have to admit that your profession doesn't make angels out of men."
Attorney: "No, Doc. You doctors have us there."

68. "Is your mother living?"
"Yes."
"Was she living five years ago?"

69. "What do you remember next, Mrs. Green?"
"The next thing I remember, sir, is your helping me out of the car after the accident."

12, 715, 860, 1088

Auction

70. A man bought a parrot after spirited bidding.
"Can he talk?"
"Who do you suppose has been bidding against you all this time?"

1388

Author

71. Actress: "I just love your book. I really enjoyed reading it. Who wrote it for you?"
Author: "I'm glad you liked my book. Who read it to you?"

72. "How many words are there in a novel?"
"Oh, about 90,000 to 95,000."
"Goody, goody. I've finished my novel."

73. George Bernard Shaw sent Winston Churchill two tickets to his new play. "Bring a friend, if you have one," Shaw wrote.
Churchill replied, "I can't go that night, but perhaps some other night, if there are any others after the opening performance."

151, 270, 809

Automobile

74. The first time I was in Los Angeles I got caught on one of those freeways. I was running low on gas. I finally edged myself to the right lane, got off, and filled up. The station attendant said, "Get back in there. You're still in third place."

75. I would drive 55 mph, but I can't stand the noise of trucks hitting my trunk.

76. On the *Today* show, April 17, 1979, police radar registered a wall going 99 mph and an air conditioner going 82 mph. Yet courts say that radar is "reasonable" evidence.

77. Have you ever noticed that empty parking spaces are always on the other side of the street? You go around the block and the parking spaces are still on the other side of the street.

78. Have you ever noticed that you never have minor problems with your car on weekends?

79. He explained how he stripped his gears this way: "A fellow pulled up alongside of me and said, 'Let's drag!' So I put it into L for leap and leaped out. Then I shifted to D for drag. Then I pushed it into R for race, and that's when something went wrong."

80. A fellow drove from New York to Los Angeles with one of those new electric cars and only used $3.12 worth of electricity. The drawback, however, was that the extension cord cost $18,789.

81. "Can I park here?"
    Cop: "No."
    "But how about all these other cars that are parked here?"
    "They didn't ask me as you did."

82. We would really conserve gas if we kept all of the cars that are not paid for off the roads.

83. VW: Germany's revenge for getting beaten in the war.

84. A red light is a place where you meet the fellow that passed you going 80 mph a little ways up the road.

85. An O-turn is a person who changed his mind after making a U-turn.

86. A motorist gave a ride to a hitchhiker. He offered the hitchhiker a smoke.
    "No, if the Lord had intended for us to smoke, he would have given us a nose with the nostrils upside-down like a chimney."
    "Well, if that's the way you feel about it, buddy, if the Lord had intended for us to ride, he would have given us wheels instead of legs. Get out!"

87. "Why didn't you give him half the road?"
    "I would have if I could have figured out which half he wanted."

88. There's only one thing on my car that doesn't make some sort of noise, and that's the horn.

89. Cop: "Pull over. You don't have a taillight."
    The motorist went into a tizzy.

Cop: "It's not all that bad. It's only a light bulb. You can get a new one at the next gas station."

"Yes, but what happened to my trailer?"

90. Motorist: A person who drives carefully after seeing an accident (pause) for at least fifteen minutes.

91. Auto dealer's ad: Come in and start something!

92. VW Rabbit: Bug's Bunny.

93. You can't say that Henry Ford didn't try. He did his darndest to turn General Motors into Colonel Motors.

1, 4, 19, 383, 447, 451, 521, 560, 613, 638, 699, 714, 798, 800, 964, 1174, 1292, 1322, 1323, 1325, 1342, 1389

Automation

94. I think they're carrying this automation thing a bit too far. I put money in the coffee machine. Out came the coffee, the cream, the sugar—but no cup. I didn't even have to drink the coffee.

Axioms

95. The nose of a hound dog is what keeps him from barking up a tree where there is no raccoon.

96. The bigger a man's head gets, the easier it is to fill his shoes.

97. Everybody is smarter than somebody, but nobody is smarter than everybody.

98. The newest thing in the world is history that hasn't been read.

99. It is good etiquette to return the book on etiquette that you borrowed.

100. Those who are successful find that before long there is decay in the processes that brought success.

101. A closed mouth gathers no feet.

102. Wet streets do not cause rain.

103. Early to bed and early to rise, and your head won't feel three times its size.

104. Nothing makes a man go places like a woman who likes to.

105. The clothes that make a woman are the clothes that break a man.

106. Experts on making love seldom read books on the subject.

107. A person is innocent until proven President.

108. You can't push something that is going faster than you are.
109. Cole's law: Thinly sliced cabbage.
110. Blind people don't join nudist colonies.
111. A rut is a grave with both ends knocked out.
112. The bigger the mouth, the better it looks shut.
113. When people despair, they either turn to apathy or violence.

B

Baby

114. "Son, this morning the stork found a beautiful baby girl among the cabbages in our garden. Why don't you write your brother at college about it?"

He did. "Dear Jack: You owe me a buck. It's a girl."

115. "The baby has my brains."

"She must have. I still have mine."

116. The baby was born on the lawn in front of the hospital, but the doctor still charged $125 for the delivery room. Understandably, the new parents objected, so the doctor changed the bill to read: "Greens fees, $125."

117. A woman got her birth control pills mixed up with her saccharin tablets. Now she has the sweetest baby you have ever seen.

221, 918, 1074, 1418

Baby Sitter

118. "Your mother and I won't be here tonight. Do you want to sleep alone or with the baby sitter?"

"What would you do, Dad?"

119. When the baby sitter calls to ask you where the champagne glasses are, it's time to go home.

Bad Luck

120. My ship finally came in, but it was just my luck that there was a dock strike and we couldn't unload.

210, 610, 1315

Bald

121. Bald man: "I'd give a lot to have just one thing. Dandruff!"

122. Bald man: A live wire with the insulation burned off.

123. A bald man is the first to find out when it is raining.

124. Bald men can take comfort in the fact that they don't put marble tops on cheap tables. Unfortunately they are to be found on antiques, though.

1253

Banker

125. Old banker's don't die. They just lose interest.

126. Some bankers are known by their deeds. Others are known by their mortgages.

127. A Chicago banking firm asked a Boston investment house for information concerning a young Bostonian the bank was considering hiring. The Boston investment firm couldn't say enough good things about the young man. His father was a Cabot. His mother was a Lowell. Aunts and uncles were Saltonstalls, Appletons, Peabodys, and Kennedys.

Several days later the investment firm heard from the Chicago bank: "The information you gave us was inadequate. We are not contemplating using the young man for breeding purposes."

209, 488

Baptist

128. A Methodist minister was asked to bury a Baptist. They had been close friends and next-door neighbors. The request was a bit unusual so the Methodist minister asked the Bishop.

The Bishop said, "By all means, bury all the Baptists you can."

129. Baptists sin just like everybody else. It's just that their religion forbids them to enjoy it.

130. There was an attempt to merge the Christian Church with the Baptist Church. One old timer said, "I was born a Baptist, I am a Baptist, and I always will be a Baptist. They're not going to make a Christian out of me."

243, 276, 277, 1136

Baptize

131. Mrs. Johnson finally got her reprobate husband to join the church. The baptizing was at the river. When the pastor dunked Jack for the first time, an ace floated out of his sleeve and floated down the river. When he was immersed a second time, another ace floated out of his sleeve and floated down the river.

"Preacher, stop the baptizin'. That man can't be saved. He can't be won."

A man on the bank said, "Mrs. Johnson, with a hand like that, I don't see how he can lose."

Baseball

132. When Joe Torre was the catcher for the Milwaukee Braves, he got into an argument with a fellow player. The other player bellowed out, "You're a chicken Catcher Torre."

133. He struck out 1,330 times, a record in futility unapproached by any other player until Mickey Mantle came along. But that is not why we remember him. We remember Babe Ruth for his 714 home runs.

134. A rookie missed two easy catches in right field. The manager was miffed to say the least. "Let me show you how to play right field."

So the manager went out and goofed twice, too. He came back with, "You've got right field so screwed up that nobody can play it."

135. "They's two chances of changing an umpire's decision; slim and none." Dizzy Dean.

136. The girls were drinking gin at the baseball game. About the fifth inning, the bags were loaded.

137. "Sometimes my amazin' ball players are really amazin.'" Casey Stengel.

138. On the first pitch of the game, the hitter hit the ball out of the park.

"You blankety-blank! You ruined my no-hitter!"

139. Someone asked him why he was such a good pitcher. He said there were three reasons:
   1. Clean living
   2. Lots of practice
   3. A good infield and outfield

140. As a shortstop, he had one weakness—the balls batted at him.

141. "Harmony is what we need. Harmony is our .300 hitter. Harmony is our clutch batter. Harmony is our twenty-game pitcher."

A rookie heard all this and asked, "If Harmony's that good, why don't we trade for him?"

142. He had three problems. He couldn't catch. He couldn't hit. He couldn't run.

143. I slid into second base. Like the deodorant ad says, I didn't want to be half-safe.

832, 842, 1115, 1122

Basketball

144. Coach: "Would you have liked me as much if we had lost?"
Owner: "Yes, but I would have missed you."

145. Referee: "Shut your mouth. If you open it once more, I'll chew your head off."

Player: "Then you'd have more brains in your stomach than you have in your head."

253, 1120, 1122

Bath

146. A woman asked for seventy-eight quarts of milk for a milk bath.
"Pasteurized?"
"No, up to my waist is enough."

369, 413, 550, 555, 630, 671, 853

Benefactor

147. His name appeared in the newspaper only twice—once when he was born and once in the obituary column. However, his influence on his fellow human beings was far greater than any activist who gets his or her name on the front page every day.

Benefit

148. Abel used an ax to benefit mankind, but Cain used it to kill. That same sort of thing is still going on today.

Bible

149. What's the world coming to? New hotels and motels chain their Gideon Bibles to the table.

150. Galileo was wrong. The earth is flat! The Bible says, "The angels were at the four corners of the earth."

151. "I don't believe in the Bible because the authors are unknown."
   "Then I'm sure you don't believe in the multiplication tables either. Nobody knows who wrote them."

31

Big is Bad

152. This "big is bad" thing isn't as new as you might think it is. Do you remember the story of Jack and the Beanstalk? Jack broke into the giant's house. That's breaking and entering. He stole the goose that lays the golden eggs. That's larceny. He chopped down the beanstalk and killed the giant. That's vandalism and murder.
   Jack was small. The giant was big. Jack pulled breaking and entering, larceny, vandalism and murder but he came out the hero of the story. The innocent giant is the villain.

Bikini

153. Nature tries to hide her mistakes, but then she puts on her bikini and blows the whole thing.

154. I wouldn't exactly say she is fat, but for a bikini she uses a hammock and two beach umbrellas.

155. A bikini is very uninteresting in itself. But give it to a shapely girl who understands how to use a bikini and you have quite another proposition.

Billiards

156. A traveling salesman was marooned in a small town during a snowstorm. There was one pool hall but the balls were all a dirty gray.
   "How can you tell the balls apart?"
   "If you keep playing, eventually you'll recognize them by their shape."

Bills

157. Just call me Bill. I was born on the first of the month.

5, 376, 399, 719, 847

Birth Control

158. "Mrs. Johnson, I've been sent to see you because you have twelve children, and I want to give you this little booklet on birth control."

"Thank you, but that might be all right for you unmarried ladies. I'm married. I don't need it."

117, 1343

Birthday

159. I like to see birthdays roll around. When they stop, I won't be with you anymore.

160. He'll be thirty-five tomorrow. Just think, in another twenty-four hours, he'll be able to take Geritol.

237, 790, 1029

Blind

161. Officer: "It must be dreadful to be lame. But it could be worse. Think of what it would be like if you were blind."

Beggar: "When I was blind, I got so many counterfeit bills."

162. "Have you been blind all your life?"

George Shearing: "Not yet."

110, 203, 550

Bowling

163. The Ministerial Association called their bowling team the Holy Rollers. You never saw so many preachers in the alley and the gutter in your life.

Boxing

164. The prize fighter stumbled back into his corner all beat up. His second told him, "Keep it up, boy. You've got a no-hitter going."

165. Joe Louis's trainer said, "Don't get up till the count of nine. Rest!"

But when Tony Galento floored Louis, he jumped right back up. He explained later, "I didn't want to give Tony nine seconds of rest."

825

Broker

166. Isn't it ironic? This guy drives up in his Lincoln Continental to get investment advice from a brokerage firm's clerk who drives a Honda.

Budget

167. "We've got money left in our budget. What should we do with it?"

"Let's build another bridge across the Mississippi."

"But there are already dozens of bridges across the Mississippi River."

"Lengthwise?"

168. A budget is a planned method of worrying.

Bull

169. Jim visited his cousin on the farm. "Why doesn't this bull have horns?"

"Well, there are several reasons. Some bulls are born without horns. Some bulls get their horns late in life. Other bulls are de-horned. However, the main reason this bull doesn't have horns is that he is a horse."

170. One bull in the pasture wanted to go to Rome to become a papal bull.

Another wanted to go to Bavaria and be a bull in a china shop.

A third bull wanted to go to Wall Street and fight the bears.

A fourth said he just wanted to stay in the pasture for heifer and heifer and heifer.

171. A big bull, a medium-sized bull, and a small bull walked along the road. The big bull jumped over the big fence. The medium-sized bull jumped over the medium-high fence. The little bull walked on.

Moral: A little bull goes a long way.

Bureaucracy

172. If the Good Lord would have wanted us to have oil, he wouldn't have given us the Department of Energy. Do you remember what it was like before the politicians were protecting us from the oil companies?

173. Never argue with a bureaucrat who buys his or her paper by the truckload.

1134

Business

174. Business is like sex. When it is good, it is very good. When it is bad, it is still pretty good.

175. "How's business?"

"Lousy! Even the deadbeats aren't coming into the store anymore."

176. Having spent a lifetime in the farm equipment business, this is the way we heard this one. Change it to whatever business fits the situation.

Dear Abby: I have two brothers. One is in the farm equipment business and the other was executed in the electric chair. My mother died in a mental institution and my father peddles drugs. My two sisters are prostitutes. Recently I met a wonderful girl who has just been released from the reformatory. I want to marry her. My problem is this: If I marry this girl, should I tell her about my brother who is in the farm equipment business? Signed, Curious.

177. A lot of people who complain about their dumb boss would be out of a job it their dumb boss were any smarter.

178. If you come up with a bad idea in business, you go bankrupt. If you come up with a bad idea in politics, you get reelected.

179. "I can get beer eight miles out of town for 25 cents a glass."

"You can't save any money by driving eight miles to get 25-cent beer."

"Yes, you can. I keep drinking until I show a profit."

180. Before you tell me how to solve the world's problems, why don't you clean up the mess in your office?

181. Don't hit a competitor when he is down—no more than six or seven times anyway.

182. He manufactures that slippery stuff that you put on napkins, to be sure that your napkin will slide off your lap.

183. He took IBM and LSD and went on a business trip.

326, 457, 475, 478, 481, 529, 546, 599, 831, 837, 838, 862, 905, 916, 927, 1057, 1086, 1137, 1169

Busing

184. "You're taking one of those learn-at-home courses, aren't you?"

"Yes."

"You'll have to take a bus to the other side of town to do your studying."

Butcher

185. "How much is that steak?"
      "$8.45."
      "But you didn't even weigh it."
      "Lady, I've weighed that steak ten times this morning."

686, 1152

C

California

186. Ah, California, where the sun shines 365 days a year, and that's a conservative estimate.

187. "What's the largest apple you ever grew in California?"
"Stop touching that grape."

188. During the earthquake, Bill's zip code changed three times before he got out of bed.

Campaign

189. A politician won an election by saying this about his opponent:
"He is a bachelor who practices celibacy. He matriculated with coeds at the university he attended. He is a shameless extrovert who practices nepotism with his brother in their shoe store. He has a sister who is a thespian on the stage at Wicket, New York."

190. There can be no doubt about it. This *is* the promised land. Every political campaign we get a set of new promises.

191. P.T. Barnum said, "You can fool all the people part of the time and part of the people all the time, but you can't fool all the people all the time."
Could be, but if you can fool enough of them you can win an election.

192. Politicians: "The role of government is to assert the national interest."
Mussolini said the very same thing but he used different words. He used Italian words.

193. Have you ever heard the phrase, "What have you done for me lately?" This is the story from which the phrase was drawn.
A voter in Kentucky told Alben Barkley that he would not vote for him in the next election.

"But I've done you a lot favors. I got your brother a job as a postmaster. I got a scholarship at the University of Kentucky for your son. I got a contract for your brother, and then got a loan for him from the government. I appointed your brother-in-law to be a federal judge."

"Yes, Alben, that's right. But what have you done for me lately?"

Canada

194. A Canadian living in Florida came home for Christmas. The Canadian customs official, noting the Florida license plate, said, "Anybody so stupid as to come up here at this time of the year from where you came from isn't smart enough to smuggle anything in. Go on through."

195. My Canadian friends tell me that they have eight months of winter and four months of tough sledding. They say that if summer comes on Sunday, they go fishing.

Cancel

196. Due to a lack of interest, tomorrow is cancelled.

8

Capital

197. Capital is lending money. Labor is getting it back.

855, 1255

Career

198. If you doubt the value of proper mate selection, consider the way Adam wrecked a promising career by marrying an ambitious apple saleswoman.

548

Cat

199. Never try to out-independence a cat.

200. Old Tom, our tomcat, travels forty-seven yards every night.

201. After old Tom was changed from a he to an it, he ran off.
    "You've lost your tomcat."
    "No, we haven't. Tom is just out changing some of his social engagements."

47, 325, 364, 482, 909, 1045

Catholic

202. On a cold day, two nuns stood in front of the Unemployment Office waiting for a bus. An employee invited the nuns inside. Two men coming into the office noticed the nuns and one said, "Look over there. If the Pope is laying them off, there sure won't be any job for us."

203. At St. Ursala's they were having a benefit for the high school band. The second act was terrific. Three nuns in the front row of the balcony got up and cheered. One got so carried away that she slipped and fell overboard. Luckily she grabbed a chandelier and swung out over the crowd.

A priest noticed this immediately. He ran to the mike and yelled, "Anybody that looks up will be struck blind."

"Mike, what are you going to do?"

"I think I'll risk one eye."

204. "Father O'Riley, something has to be done about my Sean. He doesn't come home at night. My eight kids and I are left alone while he's all over town drinking, gambling, and chasing women."

"You have my deepest sympathy, Mrs. Flanagan. Sean is a miserable sinner."

"Sinner, yes. But miserable no. He's having the time of his life."

205. I got fired from the laundry because I went to the convent and asked the Mother Superior if the nuns had any dirty habits.

206. Roman Catholics play Bingo in Latin so that Protestants can't win.

207. It was common knowledge that Pat stole lumber. Father O'Reilly said that Pat should make restitution.

Father, if you've got the blueprints for a restitution, or whatever you call it, I've got the lumber."

3, 463, 680, 728, 729, 830, 1135

Change

208. If you worry about adjusting to change, consider the adjustments the horsefly had to make some years ago.

135, 188, 201, 499, 520, 572, 588, 857, 970, 983, 1136, 1330

Charity

209. "Of the $2,500 we have in the bank, let's give $1,400 to the museum and $1,200 to the library; then let's give the $100 deficit to the Red Cross."

"How about giving 75 percent of our deficit to the Red Cross and the other 50 percent to the Salvation Army?"

Check in Mail

210. It is good news when you're told the check is in the mail. It is bad news when you find out that it was a recorded announcement.

1149

Checks and Balances

211. Our political system supposedly is one of checks and balances.

We have checks all right; relief checks, allotment checks, Social Security checks, unemployment checks, poverty checks, rent-subsidy checks.

Where are the balances?

Chicago

212. Crime is getting so bad in Chicago, the caskets now have locks on them (pause) so they can be locked from the *inside.*

213. Chicago is where the votes count and count and count and count and count and count.

1350

Chicken

214. "This is not domestic fowl. There's buckshot in it."

"That buckshot was meant for me when I grabbed the domestic fowl."

215. The little red hen is the only creature that can sit still and *still* create dividends.

132, 425, 485, 493, 498, 895, 1060, 1157

Children

216. "Do you know who this man is (pointing to Abraham Lincoln on a penny)?"

"Yeah, he's the guy that makes pennies."

217. Betsy suddenly began cleaning her usually messy room. You see, Betsy had strayed from the comic page to the police court column in the newspaper, and seen an item about a woman being jailed for running a disorderly house.

218. "Why don't you ask your mother?"
"I don't want to know that much about it."

219. Proud mother: "Just think, last week Mary Ann went to the psychiatrist all by herself."

220. In today's society, everything in the house is controlled by switches (pause) except the kids.

221. "Aren't you glad now that you prayed for a baby sister?"
Looking at his new twin sisters, the boy replied, "Yes, Dad, but aren't you glad that I quit praying when I did?"

222. "Aren't you afraid that your little boy will get squashed in this crowded elevator?"
"Not a chance. He bites."

223. Thank you, Aunt Martha, for the book *Penguins and Their Habitats*. It is a beautiful book, but it told me more about penguins than I care to know.

224. Summer is that joyous time of the year when the kids slam the doors that they left open all winter.

225. Nothing makes a child as ill-behaved as when he or she belongs to a neighbor.

226. In another week you'll be going back to school. They'll make you behave there!

227. Mother asked for a doggie bag.
"Oh, goody, goody. We're going to get a dog."

228. "Daddy, why didn't Noah swat both flies when he had a chance?"
"Go to bed, son."

229. I sure hope that when I die I'll be sound asleep because I don't want to wake anybody.

230. Do you remember that vase we've had in our family generation after generation? Well, this generation just broke it.

231. "My Dad can lick your Dad."
"That's nothing. So can my Mom."

232. A little kid boosted another so he could see over the wall of a nudist camp.
"What are they doing?"
"Playing volleyball."
"Boys or girls?"
"Can't tell. They don't have any clothes on."

233. Only good people go to heaven. Other people go where it is hot all the time, kind of like Tucson.

234. Two 12-year-olds decided to get married. They pooled their piggy-bank money and said they would live in the tree house.
"What will you do if there are children?"
"If she lays an egg, I'm going to step on it."

235. "I'll bet you don't know what the word 'expectorate' means."
"Sure do. It's slang for *spit.*"

236. "What month has twenty-eight days?"
"All twelve of them."

237. Maybe I'll be dead sometime. But I hope I don't die on my birthday because it's no fun having a birthday party when you're dead.

238. If a young person is dull at age fifteen, he or she was probably dull at age fourteen.

239. Why do people tie up their dogs but allow their kids to run loose?

240. "How come you kicked your sister in the stomach?"
"I didn't know she was going to turn around."

158, 204, 255, 261, 269, 396, 483, 489, 604, 680, 767, 1002, 1030, 1297, 1323, 1333, 1385

China

241. In China when they begin to dig a tunnel through a mountain, they don't bother with blueprints. They place people on both sides of the mountain and tell them, "Dig!" If they meet in the middle, there is one tunnel. If they don't there are two tunnels. Ah so.

902, 1380, 1391

Church

242. "Tell me, do you expect the President to be in church next Sunday?"
"That I cannot promise, but we expect God to be here, and we figure that will be incentive enough for a reasonably large attendance."

243. A Baptist church got rid of unwanted parked cars in their parking lot after they erected this sign: NO PARKING. Violators will be baptized.

244. Thursday at 7:00 p.m. there will be a meeting of the Little Mothers' Club. All ladies wishing to become mothers will please meet the pastor in the vestry after this service.

245. Church is like a filling station. You get filled up on Sunday, but by Saturday you've run dry and need to go to church again on Sunday.

246. Church sign: Come early and get a Back Seat!

247. "Everybody in this parish is going to die."
   One man laughed. "I don't belong to this parish."

248. Comfort the troubled. Trouble the comfortable. That's what church is all about.

249. A new mission was started in a barroom. When the parrot saw the preacher, he said, "New bartender." When he saw the choir, he said, "New floor show." When he saw the people, he said, "Same old customers."

250. Sign on church: God Is Alive and Well! Visiting hours twice on Sunday. 8:00 a.m. and 10:30 a.m."

251. There were so many shotgun weddings in that church that they began calling it Winchester Cathedral.

252. It's easier to learn to swim and ride a bike when you're young. It's also easier to establish spiritual disciplines.

253. Some people don't go to church because they think they are better than those who do. Imagine a basketball player refusing to play because he felt he was better than the others on the team?

254. A deaf man came to church each Sunday. He couldn't hear anything, but he wanted people to know which side he was on.

255. A hurricane shook the church . . .
   "Lord, send us the spirit of the children of Israel, the children of Moses, the children of the promised land."
   "Lord, don't you listen to Brother Johnson. You come yourself. This is no job for a kid."

256. "How tall is the church?"
   "Five and a half feet."
   "What?"
   "Well, my dad's six feet tall and he says he's had it up to here with the church."

257. Nothing tests your faith quite as much as being caught with only a twenty dollar bill when the collection plate is passed.

279, 531, 781, 1142, 1165, 1217, 1262, 1298

Churchill

258. Churchill, referring to Clement Atlee: "Clem is a modest little man who has a great deal to be modest about."

259. "We shall not flag or fail. We shall fight on the beaches, we shall fight on the landing grounds, we shall fight in the fields and in the streets, we shall fight in the hills. We shall never surrender. I have nothing to offer but blood, sweat, and tears. Let us brace ourselves for our duties, and so bear ourselves that if the British Empire and its Commonwealth last for a thousand years, men will say, 'This was our finest hour.' " Winston Churchill.

260. The English teacher says, "Do not end your sentences with prepositions," but Winston Churchill said, "This is the sort of nonsense up with which I will not put."

73, 1301

Circus

261. The invisible man in the circus married the invisible woman. Their kids weren't much to look at either, by the way.

614

Citizen

262. You can always tell a good citizen. He or she acts the same whether there is a law on the subject or not.

601   ۰

Civic Clubs

263. Rotary owns the town. Kiwanis runs the town. But it is the Lions who have all the fun.

264. A local civic club elected a new preacher in town to be "club hog caller."

He said, "I thought I would come here to be the shepherd of the flock. But if you insist that I call the hogs, that's okay with me. You know your people better than I do. I'm new here."

265. Groucho Marx was invited to join a civic club but he declined.

"I wouldn't join a club that would accept members like me."

Clergy

266. "My dear, haven't you forgotten to say the blessing?"
"If you can see any food on this table that hasn't been blessed at least three times, show me what it is."

267. The Rev. Henderson was making his Sunday afternoon calls . . .
"Pa ain't home. He went over to the country club. Oh, he didn't go over to play golf—not on Sunday. He just went over for a few drinks and a little stud poker."

268. He was talking to an English clergyman. A canon, I think; maybe a howitzer.

269. The pastor's little Cindy was sick. Her mother put her to bed.
"I want to see Daddy."
"Shush. Daddy's busy right now."
"OK, then I want to see my pastor. I'm sick."

270. The pastor's wife wrote a book: *How Green Was My Pastor.*

271. Two preachers differed on doctrinal matters.
"That's all right. We're both doing the Lord's work. You in your way, I in his way."

272. A priest gave a ride to a girl who had had too many drinks. She kept saying, "You're passionate," but the priest ignored her.
"Where do you live?"
"I've been trying to tell you. You're passin' it."

273. Two hippies got married. The clergyman couldn't tell which was male and which was female.
"Will one of you please kiss the bride?"

274. He prayed for the people in the service, but he didn't say whether it was the 9:00 a.m. service or the 11:00 a.m. service.

275. The pastor was fond of cherry brandy. A parishioner offered the pastor a fifth if he would mention it in the Sunday bulletin. The pastor accepted the challenge and the brandy. The bulletin read: "Pastor Smith thanks Brother Beavers for his gift of fruit and the spirit in which it was given."

276. Baptist ministers and Standard Oil employees were banqueting in the same hotel. The program coordinator for Standard Oil ordered a cross-slice of watermelon for dessert because the red section looked a little like a Standard Oil sign. He told the chef, "Add a little gin to each slice, please."

When it came time for dessert, the waiters took the watermelon to the Baptist ministers' banquet hall by mistake. Then the mistake was discovered.

"Go get that watermelon back quick! Quick!"

"Too late. They've already eaten it."

"What happened?"

"They seemed to like it. I saw several of them putting the seeds in their pockets."

277. Father Hannigan said he was a compulsive gambler.

Rabbi Steinberg said he was a compulsive admirer of women.

Rector Buckingham said he was a compulsive drinker.

Baptist Pastor Jones said he was a compulsive gossip.

278. The Rev. Horace H. Tweedle turned down the honorary doctorate. "I'll be darned if I want to be called Tweedle D.D. all the rest of my life," he said.

279. The Norwegian bishop inspected the church in a small town. He found things generally in order, but he added, "I found an unreasonable amount of illegitimacy in the parish."

"My dear Bishop, what would you consider a reasonable amount of illegitimacy?"

280. An eighty-year-old preacher watched a pretty girl pass.

"I never tire of looking at the fine works of God's creation," he said.

281. Pastor Franklin preached for eighty-three minutes. He had taken his wife's false teeth by mistake and couldn't stop.

282. Our preacher done absconded with the funds. But we caught up with the varmint up by Huntsville. He had spent all the money, part of it on women and the other part foolishly. We got him now and we're bringin' him back. We're going to make him preach it out.

163, 244, 249, 264, 415, 585, 613, 620, 729, 1140, 1214, 1302, 1351

Coffee Break

283. "Do you have a Sexhauer in this office?"

"Good gracious, no. We don't even get coffee breaks."

284. You are two months ahead with your coffee breaks and three months behind with your work.

22, 94, 1205

Cold

285. It was so cold the dog was pushing the fox to get him started.

478, 620, 685, 819, 1037, 1156, 1231

College

286. In a college town, an old horse pulled the milk wagon for nineteen years. When the horse retired, the college gave it an honorary degree. The horse knew the route better than the students that drove it. The horse had actually put scores of students through college.

Incidentally, this was also the first time that a whole horse got an honorary degree.

287. A speech professor told his students to stay away from hackneyed phrases. Then he asked for recitation.

First student: "The child of today will be the adult of tomorrow."

The professor jumped up and said, "You don't say. Now that is a startling observation."

288. Mary Jane handed in her speech outline.

"Professor, will this do?"

"Will it do what?"

289. A college education never hurt anyone who was willing to learn after graduation.

290. The president of the university is supposed to make speeches. The faculty is supposed to think. The deans are supposed to keep the president from thinking and the faculty from making speeches.

291. "Why didn't you answer me?"

"I did, Professor. I shook my head."

"You didn't expect me to hear it rattle clear up here, did you?"

292. Two fraternities were having a touch football game when a shapely woman walked across the field.

"Time out (pause) for measurements."

293. You can always tell a Yale man, but you can't tell him much.

294. College years: The vacation between mother and wife. (Or father and husband.)

295. Some professors make a living wage. The rest don't have a second job.

296. "You say you have a son who had to leave college because of poor eyesight?"

"Yes, he mistook the dean of women for one of the coeds."

297. A preoccupied professor came into the tonsorial/beautician emporium to have his hair cut. He sat beside a woman.

When it came time for the professor to get his hair cut, he said, "Haircut please."

The barber said, "Would you mind removing your hat?"

The professor, noticing the woman for the first time, said, "Oh, I'm sorry. I didn't know there were ladies present."

298. A freshman in a boarding school wrote her parents, "I am getting fat on the awful food we have here in the dorm. I weigh 120 pounds stripped, but I don't know whether those scales down in front of the drug store are right or not."

299. When Jack got all F's and one D, his parents asked for an explanation.

"I guess the reason I got all the F's was that I spent too much time getting that D."

300. The Tappa Keg house sent its draperies to be laundered. The windows were bare. The frat house got a letter from the sorority house across the street:

"Dear Sirs: May we suggest that you secure some draperies for your windows? We do not care for your course in anatomy. Signed, The Getta Guys."

One of the Tappa Kegs penned a note to the bottom of the letter and placed the letter in the sorority house's mailbox. The note read: "The course is optional."

301. A college freshman said, "I'll never trust my parents again. I asked them for $600 for an encyclopedia and they sent me an encyclopedia."

114, 538, 741

Committee

302. Now I'll turn you over to the rubber hose committee. They'll get you to pay your dues.

303. God so loved the world (pause) that he didn't send a committee.

659

Complaint

304. Out of the 85,000 people in that football stadium, why did that pigeon pick on me?

305. "Why do people complain about thorns among the roses? Why don't they exult over the roses among the thorns?" Benjamin Franklin.

3, 177, 321, 642, 686, 1026, 1076, 1332

Compliment

306. "You seem to have plenty of intelligence for a man in your position."

"Thank you, Your Honor, and if I wasn't under oath, I would return the compliment."

307. Compliment a women of twenty and she will blush. Compliment a women of thirty and she thinks you're clever. Compliment a woman of forty and she wonders what you want.

414

Computer

308. Princeton has a computer that measures IQ as a person asks it a question.

One person asked, "What do you think about nuclear proliferation?" The computer registered, "IQ—150."

A second person asked, "What are the chances for the Green Bay Packers?" The computer printed out, "IQ—100."

Finally, a third asked, "What's your handle, good buddy?" The computer registered, "IQ—50."

309. When the computer makes an error, there will be several human errors that led to it, including the error of blaming the whole thing on the computer.

29, 327

Conceit

310. He was so conceited, he joined the Navy so that the world could see him.

311. In my lifetime, I've been wrong only once. That was when I thought I was wrong but wasn't.

Concert

312. There is something about a concert that makes people cough.

313. We will now hear Joe Banana and his Band of Appeal.

680

Confidence

314. A man stretched a taut wire in his backyard. He practiced pushing a wheelbarrow across the wire, hoping one day to accomplish that feat over Niagara Falls. His neighbors ridiculed him, but one young lady in the community lent him encouragement.

"With your determination and patience, I know that you can do it."

"Great! I'm so glad you have that much confidence in me. I'm looking for someone to ride in the wheelbarrow as I push it over Niagara Falls."

315. He certainly is confident. He's the only man I know of who does crossword puzzles in ink.

678

Congress

316. It is not easy to sit in Congress every day. It's like having Howard Cosell for a roommate.

317. The only thing that Congress can do in thirty days is make minute tapioca.

318. "What comes after the Senator's speech?"
"Christmas."

319. "Congress is strange. A man gets up to say nothing. Nobody is there to hear him. Then everybody disagrees with him." Will Rogers.

320. When Congress is in session, you had better place your life, liberty, and pursuit of happiness in a safety-deposit box.

321. Never complain when Congress does nothing. They can't hurt you much doing nothing. It's when Congress does something that you had better watch out.

322. Don't blame Congress for being irresponsible. If you had almost a trillion dollars at your disposal and it was somebody else's money, you would be irresponsible too.

323. Congress manages to find a problem for every solution.

1045, 1289, 1295

Conservation

324. I have a great idea for saving energy. Build all roads downhill.

82

Consultant

325. The noisy old tomcat was neutered. After that he quieted down and took up work as a consultant.

326. A consultant is a person who can make more money telling you how to run your business than you can make out of it, even if you run it right instead of the way he tells you to run it.

Consumer

327. Shoppers are getting more and more sophisticated. They'll buy a cheaper cut of meat in order to save up for a TV set for the bathroom. They insist on Michigan apples, Columbian bananas, Florida grapefruit, Nebraska beef—and they get them.

Smart people, these shoppers, with their little computers hidden under their hair rollers.

503, 1261

Contrary

328. She's so contrary! When the Listerine commercial comes on, she roots for the germs.

Cooking

329. There it is dear. Cooked just like the way you'd better like it.

330. Backyard chefs should have two common props: (1) common sense, and (2) a list of nearby restaurants.

766

Courtesy

331. "How did the phrase 'ladies first' start?"

"In days of yore, when a couple came back to the cave, the cave had often been invaded by a wild animal. Hence the phrase, 'ladies first.' "

332. The sign said: Courtesy is Contagious. Some wag had written these words under the sign: "Nobody here has the disease."

Courtship

333. "Are your intentions toward our daughter honorable?"

"You mean I have a choice?"

334. If *I* had all the qualities you require in a man, I wouldn't have proposed to *you* in the first place.

335. There was more love there that night in that gathering than you can find with a police officer's flashlight.

336. I remember when boys used to chase girls. Now girls don't even run.

337. She's only a bootlegger's daughter, but I love her still.

338. Gentlemen may prefer blondes, but this blonde prefers gentlemen.

339. I'll have the oysters Rockefeller, the pressed duck, and the baked Alaska—that is, unless you're saving up for a ring or something.

340. Want ad, marked personal: "Joe, bring engagement ring, wedding ring, and teething ring. I have a surprise for you. Betty."

341. It is better to be broke than never to have loved at all.

342. You look at a potential husband the same way that you look at a house. You don't see it as it is, but as it will be after you get it remodeled.

343. A girl and a boy went out into the beautiful woods to pick flowers. There were so many people out there in the woods that they had to pick flowers.

344. "Hey, you down there! Do you think you can stay all night?"
    "Gosh. Thank you. I'll call my folks first to find out if it is okay with them too."

345. "I know he's rich, but he's too old to be eligible."
    "Dear, he's too eligible to be old."

346. If a fellow wears an ill-fitting sweater that his girlfriend knitted for him, his chances of escaping marriage can be put conservatively at 100 to 1.

347. "Where have you been all my life?"
    "The first forty years I wasn't even born."

348. "What do you give a man who has everything?"
    "Encouragement."

349. "Why did you break up with Maggie?"
    "She kept using four-letter words."
    "Maggie O'Toole? Using four-letter words?"
    "Yeah, words like don't, stop, and won't."

350. You look like the outdoor type of girl. Let's go out on the patio.

351. Father: "You can't marry my daughter."
Suitor: "Why not?"
Father: "She's a minor."
Suitor: "Great Scott, don't tell me I have to get permission from the United Mine Workers union?"

352. Mother: "I don't believe Mary's boyfriend is what we thought he was."
Father: "What's the trouble now?"
Mother: "He hung his hat over the keyhole."

353. "I won't marry you until you have saved up $1,000."
After a year . . .
"How much have you saved?"
"$35."
"That's close enough."

Credit

354. I'm such a poor credit risk they won't even take my cash.

5, 820, 1265

Credit Card

355. Everything is credit cards nowadays. The other day I paid cash and the cashier wanted to see my driver's license.

356. Definition of credit card: Instant debt!

357. I went on a trip last week and forgot my credit cards. Luckily, I finally found a motel and restaurant that would take cash.

358. My wife is in plastic surgery having her credit cards removed.

760

Crime

359. I'm not worried about crime in the streets. Out our way criminals make house calls.

360. He stole a fire truck and was arrested by a guy who had stolen a police car.

361. The girl kangaroo said her pockets had been picked.

362. In an alley, one man slashed another with a razor.
"Ha! You never touched me.'
"Try moving your head."

212, 716, 1027

Culture

363. You are cultured if you can listen to the "William Tell Overture" without thinking about the Lone Ranger.

Curiosity

364. They say, "Curiosity killed the cat," but what did the cat want to know?

Currency

365. Americans are woefully weak in geography. If you don't believe it, the next time you go to a cashier, ask, "Do you take Hawaiian currency here?"
    Let me know the answer you get.

Customers

366. A businessman drove away a salesman by saying, "I don't like you. I don't like your store. I don't like your products. Git! Do you hear me? Git!"
    "Brother, I wish I had a hundred customers like you," replied the salesman.
    "Why?"
    "Because I've got a thousand customers just like you."

249, 327, 430, 435, 608, 678, 1005, 1219

D

Dating

367. Going out with him is like being caught in a phone booth with a python.

368. "He dresses well."
   "And fast, too."

846, 1196

Daughter

369. Mother and little daughter were bathing together.
   "Mommy, how come I'm so plain and you're so fancy?"

370. Lucy always introduced herself as Lucy Jones, Judge Jones's daughter. Her mother said she should go it on her own. "Forget the 'Judge Jones's daughter.' "
   Lucy accepted the suggestion. After that she said, "I always thought I was Judge Jones's daughter, but Mom said not to say that anymore."

371. Mixed emotions: When your daughter comes home at 4:00 a.m. with a Gideon Bible under her arm.

372. "I'll bet you are a great help to your mother.'
   "Oh, yes. And so is my sister Ethel. Today it's her turn to count the spoons after the company leaves."

373. Cindy was naughty at the table so her mother told her to eat by herself at a little table in the corner. Cindy prayed, "I thank thee Lord for preparing a table before me in the presence of mine enemies."

374. Jenny stole her mother's girdle, but didn't have guts enough to wear it.

333, 604, 741, 1158, 1182, 1191, 1311

Dead

375. "Sorry to hear that you buried your wife."
"Had to. Dead, you know."

125, 229, 237, 247, 387, 398, 399, 498, 512, 560, 561, 671, 676, 682, 695, 725, 748, 773, 865, 909, 961, 1076, 1109, 1201, 1271, 1295, 1371

Debt

376. "What do you think about the abortion bill?"
"I think if we owe it, we should pay it."

834

Dentist

377. Young dentists, who are just out of dental school, have too many expectorations.

378. Dentist: Damn yanker!

379. Life as a dentist can be filling.

380. My dentist is honest, I'll say that for him. He looked into my mouth and said, "It would be cheaper if you hired a dog to do your chewing for you."

381. Her upper plate came out in the conversation.

382. Her teeth were like her pearls—false!

Depression

383. When I was a kid we had no shoes to wear and our clothes were hand-me-downs. We had little food to eat, and no car to put gas in even if we had had money for gas. Then came the Depression and things really got tough.

384. The Depression wouldn't have been so bad if it hadn't have come right smack in the middle of hard times.

1027

Desertion

385. "D'ya know, Mrs. 'Arris, I sometimes wonder if me 'usband's grown tired of me."
"Whatever makes you say that, Mizz 'Iggins?"
"Well, he aint' been 'ome for seven years."

1011

Despondent

386. She's so despondent. She looks like she went to the reading of a will (pause) and lost.

Despot

387. At the end of the Christmas story, there are the words, "They are dead who sought the young child's life."
Life is like that. Despots all finally die, thank God!

Diet

388. New diet: Eat all you want each meal, but eat breakfast on Monday, lunch on Wednesday, and dinner on Friday.
389. I'm on a reducing diet. Porterhouse steak three times a day. In two weeks, I've lost $200.

450

Direction

390. A grasshopper is hell for distance but not much for direction.

901, 1117

Dispute

391. It's a good thing there weren't two Good Samaritans. They would have argued whether the wine or the oil should be administered first.

Divorce

392. His wife divorced him because of flat feet. His feet were in the wrong flat.
393. "I want a divorce."
   "You've got grounds?"
   "Yeah, 81 acres north of town."
   "No, I mean, do you have a grudge?"
   "Yeah, I got a grudge on the farm—a two-car grudge."
394. "Isn't there a way to get out of paying alimony?"
   "Sure, there are two ways: (1) stay married, and (2) stay single."

1068, 1412

Doctor

395. "How much do you charge for house calls?"
"$50."
"How much do you charge for office calls?"
"$25."
It was 3:00 a.m. She said, "See you in your office in ten minutes."

396. Doctor: "I don't like the looks of your husband."
Wife: "Neither do I, but he's good to the kids."

397. My doctor is so expensive that I'll only call him when I think I have a terminal illness.

398. Some doctors tell you that you have pneumonia and you die of smallpox. If my doctor says, "It's pneumonia," you'll die of pneumonia.

399. "But Doc, I'm hard up. I can't pay that bill of yours."
"Well, can you pay me a quarter of what you said you would pay me if I kept you from dying?'"

400. He was so poor he had to have his tonsils taken out one at a time. When he couldn't pay for the second operation, Doc put both tonsils back in.

401. I've got a good doctor. When I broke my leg, he showed me how to limp.

402. "I've examined you, and you have locked bowels."
"But Doc, I've been in and out of the bathroom all week."
"See, what did I tell you? Yours are locked open."

403. "Have you ever had this ailment before?"
"Yes."
"You've got it again."

404. "Your heart is very sound. With a heart like that, you should have no trouble living until you are 80."
"But Doc, I'm 82 right now."
"See, what did I tell you?"

405. Doc gave me six months to live. When I couldn't pay, he gave me another six months.

406. I went to see Doc Nelson about laryngitis. He was successful. Within two weeks, I got it.

407. "I've found a satisfactory way to take cod-liver oil."
Doctor: "How is that?"
"With a fork."

56, 67, 116, 439, 475, 583, 584, 628, 682, 730, 774, 819, 858, 870, 909, 1018, 1054, 1231, 1234, 1280, 1281, 1387

Dog

408. Sign in vet's office: True love is spending $50 for an operation on a $5 dog.

95, 227, 239, 285, 380, 484, 621, 756, 761, 822, 838, 886, 893, 926, 1014, 1178, 1222, 1236, 1263, 1366

Dresses

409. The hostess chose a blue velvet gown with a low neckline for entertaining.

410. A German by the name of Seymour Heine invented the miniskirt.

411. The neckline on women's dresses is getting lower and lower. I don't know where it eventually will end, but I sure want to be there when it happens.

412. Women are competing to see who can get the most out of an evening gown.

368, 755, 757, 764, 1076, 1363, 1383, 1389

Drinking

413. "But your Honor, I had only one drink."
"From a glass or a bathtub?"

414. While on a hunting trip, a drunk lay in the bottom of the boat and shot up at a lone duck flying overhead. He got the duck. When his friends complimented him, the drunk said, "In a flock like that, I generally get six or eight."

415. At the funeral service, the preacher intoned, "The Lord giveth, the Lord taketh away. Blessed be the name of the Lord."
A drunk, hearing this, said, "If that ain't a fair proposition, I've never heard of one."

416. I gave up drinking. I saw the handwriting on the floor.

417. "I can't imagine why you bid no trump when I had three aces and four kings."
"I did it on one queen, two jacks, and three highballs."

418. Two men had "just one" in sixteen bars. Then they returned to their hotel. They crawled into bed together. Each said, "There's another guy in my bed." In the ensuing brawl, both men landed on the floor.
One drunk said to the other, "Did your man kick you out of bed too? Forget about it. Let's sleep together in the other bed."

419. Years ago a wizened rancher rode a train across the Western prairies. He went into the next car and said, "Anybody in this car have a drink? A woman fainted in our car."

Another rancher produced a hip flask and handed it to the questioner who promptly took off the cap, took two big swigs, heaved a sigh, smacked his lips, put the cap on the flask, handed the flask back to the rancher, and said, "Thanks, Mister. It sure makes me nervous to see a woman faint."

420. "Shay, can you tell me (hic) who runs Alcoholics Anonymous around here?" the drunk said.

"Why, do you want to join?"

"Course not. I want to resign."

421. Mama, Daddy and I stopped on our way home. I had a Coke and Daddy had a glass of water with an olive in it.

422. On the way home, the drunk fell on his bottle. When he got home he entered the house quietly, then went to a mirror to put Band-Aids on his cuts.

The next morning his wife accused him of being drunk the night before, a charge he vehemently denied. He wondered what made her think that he was drunk.

"There are Band-Aids all over the full-length mirror in the clothes closet."

423. Two men who had been celebrating started home. One asked the other, "Won't your wife hit the ceiling when you get home tonight?"

"She probably will. She's an awfully poor shot."

424. When he cut his finger, it bled pretty badly. Cleared up his eyes though.

425. "I've got a stewed chicken on the stove."

"That ought to sober her up."

426. Whiskey makes you fight and cheat and steal. It makes you shoot the landlord (pause) and miss.

427. He was a test pilot for Seagrams.

428. The elderly man was told he should stop drinking or he would lose his hearing. He kept drinking. He explained, "What I been drinkin' is so much better than what I been hearin', so let 'er go."

429. Flight Attendant: "Would you like a drink?"

Passenger: "Yes."

Woman sitting next to this male passenger: "No! I would rather commit adultery than drink."

Passenger: "If we have that choice, I'll skip the drink."

430. He didn't have a single steady customer in his bar.

431. He came home at 3:00 a.m. because that was the only place in town that was open.
"Drunk again!" his wife roared.
"Sho am I."

432. Where you find four salesmen, you'll also generally find a fifth.

433. Two drunks were walking the railroad tracks.
"Gosh, these steps are short."
"It's the low railings that bother me the most."

434. "Are you going to have another, Mabel?"
"No, that's just the way my coat is buttoned."

435. "Give me a 10-2 martini."
"Never heard of it. What is it?"
"Ten shots of gin and two of vermouth." The customer placed a $20 bill on the bar. The bartender, being a good businessman, began obliging the customer. He placed ten shots of gin in the shaker with two shots of vermouth. He was just about to add a few drops of lemon juice from lemon peel, when the customer remonstrated, "Hold it! If I had wanted lemonade, I would have ordered it."

436. I saw Exxon's lube engineer in the bar last night and, man was he well lubricated!

437. My grandfather is 86 years old and still doesn't use glasses. Drinks straight out of the bottle.

438. He went on the wagon (pause) for a boring ten minutes.

439. I went to one doctor and he told me to quit drinking. I went to another doctor and he told me to keep on drinking. I took the advice of the latter doctor. I like a man with guts.

440. Drunk in a phone booth: "Number hell! I want my peanuts."

441. Coach Jackson wondered why his losing team was enjoying losing so much. Then he discovered olives in the water bucket.

442. Mabel tried to get her husband to quit drinking. She dressed up like the devil to scare the living daylights out of him. When Joe came home after making his usual rounds, she jumped out and screamed. He took it all in stride. "You can't scare me. I married your sister."

443. A liquor taster said he could identify every drink by its taste. Someone slipped him a glass of water.
"I don't know what this is, but I know it won't sell."

444. He was killed by royalty: Lord Calvert.

445. First polar explorer: "It's thirty-below up here. Why don't you wear ear muffs?"

Second explorer: "I haven't worn ear muffs since my accident."
"What accident?"
"Somebody offered me a drink and I didn't hear him."

446. A drunk at the bar told the bartender, "Set 'em up for the house."
The bartender did as he was told. But the drunk didn't have any
money so the bartender kicked the drunk out in the street.

The next day the same drunk came back into the same bar. "Set 'em
up for the house! Everybody but you, bartender. You get nasty when
you drink."

49, 94, 136, 179, 204, 267, 272, 275, 277, 685

Driving

447. My wife is having a little trouble learning how to drive our car.
She went through a fence, made tracks across the neighbor's lawn,
hit a fire hydrant, jumped the curb across the street and mowed down
four mail boxes, ran over a scooter and two bicycles, narrowly missed
two pedestrians, and then the car went out of control.

448. She made a U-turn in a car wash.

449. They taught me parallel parking today. There's nothing to it.
You back into the space until you hit the car in back and then you pull
up until you hit the car in front.

1, 19, 52, 90, 166, 366, 591, 613, 697, 798, 1035, 1389

Drug Store

450. In the drug store, I weighed myself on the scale next to the soda
fountain. I weighed 115. Then I weighed myself again on the scale
next to the diet pills. I weighed 130.

451. A man dashed into a drug store, asked for a cure for hiccups.
The druggist slapped the man twice.
    "Your hiccups gone?"
    "I didn't have them. My wife out in the car has them."

298, 575, 873

Dry Cleaner

452. He was a dry cleaner who worked on the same spot for fifteen
years.

E

Economist

453. He's a great economist. He predicted nine out of the last four recessions.

454. Socialism: You give one of your two cows to your neighbor.
Communism: You give both of your cows to the government.
Capitalism: You sell one cow and buy a bull.

Education

455. Education: What you have left over after you subtract what you have forgotten from what you have learned.

289, 474

Efficiency Expert

456. An efficiency expert walking through an office saw a fellow smoking a cigarette, with his feet up on the desk, no tie, shirt tail hanging out, and hair uncombed.
"What are you doing here?" the expert asked.
"Nothing."
"How much do you make a week?"
"$200."
"When is your week up?"
"Friday."
"You don't have to wait until Friday. You're fired. Here, take this slip to the paymaster's office and get your $200."
The man left.
"By the way, who was that guy I just fired?"
"I don't know. He works for our office supply house. He delivers office supplies here every week or two."

49

457. An efficiency expert is a person smart enough to tell you how to run your business but too smart to start a business of his own.

1024, 1046

Election

458. The Promising Season ends on election eve. That's when the Alibi Season opens—the very next day.

178, 189, 191, 193, 680, 982, 1212

English

459. When an American hears a story, he will smile and laugh once. When an Englishman hears a story, he will laugh twice—once when he hears the story and once when he gets the drift of it.

460. At Queen's Hospital, young Feverisham received the glorious news that he was the father of triplets.
   Nurse: "Which two do you want to keep?"
   "I want to keep them all. What do you mean?"
   "You shall not keep them all, Mr. Feverisham. Under present British rules, one must be set aside for export."

461. When Bob Hope told an English story, someone in the crowd shouted, "But I'm English."
   "Okay, then I'll tell it a little slower."

546, 1063, 1104, 1117, 1353

Entrepreneur

462. Joe was a likable young chap who had not been blessed by the Almighty with a high IQ. The merchants around the town square thought it a Good Samaritan act when they hired Joe to shine the cannon on the courthouse lawn for a little spending money. Joe performed his task with admirable zeal, but after a year and a half, he told the merchants he was quitting.
   "I've saved up a little of the money you gave me each week. Now I've bought my own cannon and will go into business for myself."

182

Episcopal

463. Episcopalian: A nonunion Roman Catholic.

Epitaph

464. Epitaph on the tombstone of a woman who enjoyed very bad health all her life: See, I told you I was sick.

1405

Equal Rights

465. Equal rights speaker: "We have Mr. and Mrs. Egbert Wollenschmidt with us this evening. Not necessarily in that order, of course."

Eternity

466. Human reason cannot understand eternity, but think of it as a teen-ager using the telephone.

Executive

467. As everyone knows, an executive has practically nothing to do except to decide what has to be done, tell somebody to do it, listen to the reasons it should not or cannot be done that way, listen to why it should be done by somebody else or done a different way, follow up to see if the thing has been done, discover that it has not been done, inquire why, listen to excuses from the person who should have done it, follow up again to see if the thing has been done, only to discover that it has been done . . . incorrectly.

468. A prominent executive phoned from a mental institution. He had difficulty getting his party.
"Operator, do you know who I am?"
"No, I don't. But I know where you're calling from."

469. "I have no experience, but I'd like a job in the executive line. A vice presidency, for instance."
"But we already have twelve vice presidents."
"That's all right. I'm not superstitious."

1313

Exercise

470. "When I wake up each morning, I always do my exercises. I tell myself sternly, 'Ready now. Up—down—up—down.' After three strenuous minutes of this, I then do the same thing with my other eyelid." Jackie Gleason.

471. I keep my weight down by exercising. Every morning, when I wake up, I touch my shoes twenty-five times. Then I get up and put them on.

472. The only exercise I get is running out of money.

949

Expense Book

473. Let me explain the difference between a fixed cost and a variable cost. Take your expense account, for example. Travel is a fixed cost that cannot be changed. The rest is all variable. It all depends on who she is and how expensive she is.

Experience

474. Education is reading the fine print. Experience is not reading it.

469

F

Facts of Life

475. A man asked a doctor friend to tell his son about the facts of life. After the son returned from the doctor's office . . .

"Are there any questions, son?"

"Yes, Dad. What do I want to know about all that stuff? I'm going into the real estate business when I grow up."

Failure

476. He's not a failure. He just started at the bottom of the ladder and liked it there. He sits there watching the turtles whiz by.

477. He didn't have a complex. He really was inferior.

478. One bum to another: "This business isn't what it's cracked up to be. Sleeping on park benches or in cold barns. Riding freight trains and getting knocked around by railroad dicks. Never knowing where your next meal is coming from."

"Well, if you don't like it, why don't you get a job?"

"What! And admit that I'm a failure?"

259, 927, 955, 971

Family

479. I liked the dinners that came with radio better than the ones that now come with TV.

480. It's hard to raise a family, especially in the morning.

481. My folks were in the iron and steel business. My mother ironed and my dad stole.

230, 596, 604, 661, 796

Farm

482. Ranches are so far apart in Montana that every ranch has to have its own private tomcat.

483. A kid in school was asked, "What's agriculture?"
"It has something to do with farming, only farming is doing it."

484. Farmers have a constant battle with the weather. First, it's so dry in the Southwest that there are cracks in the ground six inches wide. You can drop a chain down the crack and hear it rattle for five minutes. The trees in Oklahoma lean toward the dogs. Catfish in a Texas river are two years old, and they still haven't learned how to swim. Rain has only 30 percent moisture. I was in Ames when they had that terrible drought in central Iowa a few years ago. A farmer told me, "They had rain down at Creston, but I didn't go down to watch it."

Then it turns wet in Indiana and you need a life-raft with your tractor or combine. You have to wear boots just to look out the window. The Red Cross warns on Indianapolis TV that we shouldn't plow until an hour after we get done eating. Farmers have to jack up their cows to milk them. I had a farmer at Lebanon tell me, "I had a bucket without a bottom hanging on a fencepost. Believe it or not, last Friday that bucket was half full of water."

485. "What was that big explosion over at the Webster place?"
"Jess bought some of that 'lay or bust' feed and some of his roosters got into it."

486. He put his tractor in reverse and unplowed five acres before he could get the darn thing stopped.

487. Come over and take a look at my three-year-old yearlings.

488. A gentleman farmer has more hay in the bank than he has in the barn.

489. A pitch man at the fair said he had the world's most valuable bull. "Come inside and see him for $2."
A farmer with ten kids stood, listening and looking.
"Aren't you going to come in and see the prize bull?"
"No, can't afford it with these ten kids of mine."
"They all yours?"
"Every one of them."
"Come on in free. I want my bull to take a look at you."

490. Jim planned to speed up his apple-picking chore. He placed a pulley in the top of the tree and slipped a rope through it. The rope had a barrel at one end, and was anchored to a tractor at the other

end. Jim filled the barrel with apples. When he came down to untie the rope, the heavy barrel of apples threw Jim in the air conking him on the head as it came down.

When the barrel hit the ground, the bottom came out of it. Now the barrel was lighter than Jim, so up goes the barrel and down comes Jim. Once again he got battered by the barrel. When Jim hit the ground, he let go of the rope and now the barrel came down and hit him a third time.

"The principle is all right, but I have a few details to work out," he said.

491. Mary was the most cantankerous woman in the neighborhood. I hired her to stand in my corn field to act like a scarecrow. She not only kept the crows away, they brought back the corn they had stolen the year before.

492. Jack plowed with a bull. He wanted to show the critter that life isn't all romance and tearing down fences.

493. Two maiden ladies ordered a thousand hens and a thousand roosters.

"But you don't need a thousand roosters for a thousand hens."

"You keep your nose out of our business. We know what it is to be lonely."

494. Farmer: Pitch-fork matador.

495. People want pork chops, but they don't like the smell of pigs.

496. An urban organic farming nut bought himself a few acres that he planned to farm "nature's way."

He asked a neighbor about horse eggs. The neighbor painted a couple of watermelons and sold them as horse eggs for $10 apiece. On the way home, the watermelons fell off the back of the pickup. When they hit the road, they burst open and two jack rabbits jumped out of the bush.

"It's just as well. Those horses would have been too fast to plow with anyway," he said.

497. Hired man: "I'm quitting. I have a guilty conscience."

"Over what?"

"I'm cheating two full-grown mules out of a job."

498. On a Russian collective farm, 5,000 chickens were planted head down. They died. Then 5,000 chickens were planted head up. They also died. The manager of the collective farm wrote the University of Moscow for advice.

"Please send us a soil sample," was the reply.

499. A farmer with a watermelon patch had trouble with boys stealing his melons. Finally he placed this sign in the field: One watermelon in this patch is poisoned. The next morning, when he came out to look at his melons, he noticed that the sign had been changed to read: Two watermelons in this patch are poisoned.

500. A farmer wanted to get on the party line, but two women neighbors were exchanging recipes. He yelled, "Your beans are burning!" and got the line.

501. Dairy farming is like being in jail, only in jail you don't have to milk cows.

502. American agriculture is always in a crisis of abundance. Thank the Good Lord! If you're going to have a crisis, that's the kind to have.

503. The American consumer can be thankful that farmers have not yet learned about 40-hour weeks, 8-hour days and 3-day weekends; that they haven't placed a second man in the tractor cab like the railroads have.

504. Mrs. Barnes had us over for Thanksgiving dinner. She used that new recipe for stuffing made out of popcorn. You place the stuffing in the turkey, sew the turkey up, place him in the oven and when the bunghole blows out, you know the turkey is done.

505. There is a new pesticide out for flies. It doesn't kill the flies, but it makes them sexy and you can swat two of them at a time.

506. When farm prices go down, farmers get an inverse thrill.

507. We didn't have a scale so we weighed our hogs by putting them on one end of a plank that was teetered on the gate. Then we loaded the other end with rocks until the scale balanced. Then we guessed the weight of the rocks.

508. A baker suspected a farmer of giving him short weight on butter, so he hauled the farmer into court.
    In court, the farmer placed his pound of butter on one end of the scale and a pound-loaf of the baker's bread on the other.

169, 393, 567, 608, 687, 711, 972, 1165, 1177

Fast Foods

509. Are you a quarter-pounder person?

1332

Federal Aid

510. Federal Aid: A system of making money taken from taxpayers look like a gift when part of it is handed back again.

Fed Up

511. The cannibal was fed up with people.

Fertilizer

512. Old fertilizer men don't die. They just smell that way.

671

Fight

513. She joined the Peace Corps. She's going to show the Mau Mau how to fight dirty.

514. "How'd you make out in that fight with your wife the other night?"
    "She came crawling to me on her knees."
    "Yeah? What'd she say?"
    "Come out from under that bed, you coward."

515. His nose was broken in two places. That'll teach him to stay out of those two places.

259, 426, 619, 684, 777, 843, 851

Filling Station

516. Margie: "My new boyfriend tells me he is a petroleum-transfer engineer. His name is Joe."
    Phyllis: "Oh, I know that Joe. He pumps gas at the gas station at Fifth and Main."

74, 89, 245, 1157, 1221

Fireman

517. Our volunteer firemen weren't having much success selling tickets to their dance until they placed this sign over the fire station door: Come to our dance and we'll come to your fire.

952, 1132, 1222

First Class

518. Mrs. Astorbilt had a suite on the top deck of the *Titanic*. She didn't arrive at her destination, but as far as she went, she went first class.

Fishing

519. He went ice fishing and came home with fifty pounds of ice.

520. I was ice fishing and wasn't getting a nibble. I noticed that another fellow close to me was pulling them in right and left. I moved closer to him, but that didn't change my luck. I asked him how he did it. He mumbled something I couldn't understand, so I asked again.

He took something out of his mouth and said, "You gotta keep your worms warm."

521. We had a legendary catfish that I finally hooked. But I didn't land him because he pulled me out of the boat, into a submerged car, and rolled the windows up. There is where the divers found the two of us.

522. He uses a rubber ruler to measure his fish.

523. I quit my job as a hunting guide and became a fishing guide. Fishermen never mistake you for a fish.

524. "Trout! Trout this long. I never saw such fish."
"No, I don't suppose you did."

525. The fish were on vacation the same week we were.

526. The fish we caught was so big that the picture of him weighed seven pounds.

195, 945, 1142

Florida

527. A man taking a boat trip in the Everglades was intrigued by the alligators.
"Is the alligator an amphibious creature?"
"Amphibious, hell. That fellow would take a leg off of you in a minute."

194, 1379

Florist

528. When our farm equipment dealer dedicated his new building out on the highway, he was taken aback by a wreath of flowers that had a card attached: "Sincerest condolences."

Our dealer called the florist, wondering who was pulling his leg.

"It was no gag. Would you believe there is a funeral being held in this town at this very moment that has a bouquet of flowers labeled, 'Good luck in your new location'?"

529. A flower vendor's business increased when he put up this sign: "This gardenia will make you feel important all day for only 50 cents."

Flu

530. Symptoms of swine flu: 1. Headaches. 2. Fever. 3. Desire to make love in the mud.

Followers

531. "What's that plaque next to the pulpit?"

"That is for those of our dear departed followers who died in the service."

"Which service? The 9:00 a.m. or the 10:30 service?"

606, 1085

Fool

532. P.T. Barnum said, "You can't fool all the people all the time." Maybe not, but it's a great target for politicians to shoot for.

191, 282, 751, 875, 1066

Football

533. The coach coached from the sidelines. The referee warned him, but the coach kept it up. The referee stepped off five yards.

"But the penalty for that is fifteen yards."

"The way you're coaching, five yards is enough."

534. A football coach cut down on fumbles when he made each man who fumbled last Saturday carry a football with him wherever he went during the following week.

535. "My son fixes teeth. He makes $50,000 a year."

"My son fixes brains. He makes $200,000 a year."

"My son fixes football games. He makes $1,000,000 a year."

536. The referee kicked the quarterback out of the game because he stepped on a pipe. I know. It was my pipe—my windpipe.

537. He was a triple-threat man. He could kick, run and pass (pause) exams.

538. A football player was given a special makeup exam.
"Name one means of transportation."
Silence reigned!
"How did you ever get to college, pray tell me?"
"On a scholarship."

539. And then there's the old classic . . .
"Give the ball to Calhoun. Give the ball to Calhoun."
"Calhoun say he don't want the ball."

540. "Aren't you the center on the football team?"
"Yes, Your Honor."
"How good a player are you?"
"The best the school has ever had."
Later the center explained what might have sounded like immodesty. "I was under oath. I had to tell the truth."

541. Australian football is a cross between slaves being thrown into the Coliseum and a riot in an Irish pub.

542. Tech was playing State. Tech didn't hear the whistle for the half. They kept on playing clear through the halftime break. They didn't score, but they made two first downs.

543. The play was a disorganized T with the coach in motion.

544. A football fan went to sleep on the couch while watching a game on TV. The next morning his wife awakened him. "Honey, it's twenty to seven," she said.
"Who's ahead?"

545. Father knew Joe would be a football player. When Joe was born, Dad said, "That's the end!"

292, 304, 653, 1122

Foreign Trade

546. "What do you use for fuel?"
"Sometimes wood. Sometimes coal. But mostly we burn those catalogs American companies send us. They're written in English, which our people can't understand."

727

Fortune

547. "Can I make a small fortune here?"
"Yes, if you come with a big fortune."

1398

Foul-Up

548. When John was in high school he got a small part in the senior play. There was only one line. When the cannon went off, John was to say, "Hark, the cannon."

John rehearsed his line over and over again. "*Hark*, the cannon." "Hark, the *Cannon*." John put his whole self into this part because he felt this would be the beginning of a great theatrical career.

The career foundered on opening night. When the cannon went off, John exclaimed, "What the hell was that?"

549. There was an unscheduled crash backstage while Mary was on-stage. Unrehearsed, Mary said, "We must have some mice back there."

550. A man pounded on the door, saying, "I'm your blind man." Since he was blind, Mrs. Jones came down out of the bathtub in the "all together."

This surprised the blind man. He exclaimed, "I'm your blind man. I came to put up the Venetian blinds."

551. The sign on the door said "Women." I went in and sure enough, there they were.

552. A girl with hay fever placed two handkerchiefs in her bosom. Looking for a clean handkerchief, she reached left, then right. Everybody watched.

"I'm sure I had two when I came in here."

553. A woman came up to me and tied her horse to me, thinking I was a hitching post. Then a dog came up and made the same mistake.

554. We all make mistakes, but General Custer and the captain of the *Titanic* sure made a couple of beauts.

134, 138, 205, 230, 244, 276, 365, 381, 451, 453, 528, 542, 607, 1113, 1115

French

555. French for "cut the grass": Mou d' lawn.
French for "dark bathroom": Jeanne d'Arc.
Italian for "refrigerator": Icebox.
German for "brassiere": Keepinsiefromfloppin.

556. Air France hired a girl in Memphis and taught her to answer the phone. "Bon jour, Monsieur (Madame). Air France." She got the hang of it after a few days of practice. But old habits die hard. One day she

answered the phone with, "Bon jour, Madame! Air France. Wad y'all want?"

741, 1041, 1353

Friend

557. "What do you do about snake bite out here?"
    "Carry a knife, make a small incision, suck the venom out, and spit it out."
    "But what if a person gets bit in the rear end?"
"That's when you find out who your tried and true friends really are."

73, 128, 414, 611, 680, 911, 923, 938, 942, 1080, 1100

Frugal

558. "I have heard that your wife is very frugal."
    "Yes, between the two of us, we manage to go without practically everything I need."
559. She's stingy. She fries her bacon in Woolite so it won't shrink.

Funeral

560. Two women waited for a long funeral procession to pass.
    "Who died?"
    "I don't know, but I suppose it was the person in the front car."
561. The village hellion died and was being buried. During the funeral service there was a terrific clap of thunder.
    "Well, she got there all right."

415, 528, 1102

Fur Coat

562. You don't need a mink coat. Skunk will keep you just as warm. The only creature that needs a mink coat is a mink.

563. She said she would do anything for a fur coat and now that she has one, she can't button it.

7, 709, 769, 787, 1173

Furniture

564. Their furniture goes back to Louis XIV. Louis is repossessing the furniture on the fourteenth of next month.

1161

G

Gamble

565. RAF fliers were training at a Texas base. One night five of them were playing poker. An American orderly stood watching the game.

One of the players opened with, "One pound." The man next to him was called to the phone, so the black orderly picked up the hand.

"I don't know what kind of money you're betting, but I raise you one ton."

566. Years ago, if you wanted a horse to stand still, you tied him to a hitching post. Today all you have to do is place a bet on him.

567. A farm boy spent $80 throwing hoops over bottles at the fair, and won nothing.

"Oh well, easy come, easy go. I earn my money the easy way—plowin' and milkin.' "

568. Grandma is still at her spinning wheel. Last night she won $500 on the red.

114, 204, 277, 698, 856

Genius

569. His spark of genius developed ignition trouble.

570. He had the genius of compressing a minimum of thought into a maximum of words.

1066

German

571. Heinie and Otto were pulling a buck out of the Wisconsin woods by its hind legs. A hunter came along and said, "Why don't you pull him by the antlers? He'll pull easier that way."

"Vot dos dat dumkopf know?"

"Vell, Otto, maybe he knows someding. Vy doan ve try it?"

They pulled by the antlers, and now Heine said, "See Otto, it pulls a lot easier dis vay. He's a pretty schmart young feller."

"Ya, it pulls easier, but ve're gettin' farder and farder from da pickup all da time."

572. The German Army was a long way from the supply train. Herr Kapitan told his troops, "I know dot you iss vanting a change in clothes. Ve is today going to get a change in undervear. Schultz, you change mit Schmidt. Schmidt, you change vit Untermier . . ."

83, 555, 1354

Gift

573. "Honey, do you know what day this is?"

He didn't, but to play it safe, on the way home from the office, he bought roses.

"Dear, this is the loveliest Ground Hog Day I have ever had. Thaaank you!"

574. "I want to select a gift for a wealthy aunt who is very weak and can hardly walk."

"How about some floor wax?"

510, 769, 1205

Girl

575. Mr. Wood and Mr. Stone stood on a street corner when a pretty girl walked by. Wood turned to Stone. Stone turned to Wood. They both turned to rubber. And the girl turned into a drug store.

576. A girl is judged by the company she keeps (pause) at a distance.

577. Interim Place is a halfway house for girls who don't want to go all the way.

578. I'm old enough to know the score and young enough to want to get into the game.

15, 41, 114, 155, 176, 232, 272, 280, 292, 298, 336, 343, 346, 361, 552, 556, 614, 643, 746, 844, 845, 846, 878, 1009, 1048, 1174, 1384, 1407, 1418, 1420

Goal

579. If you have set a goal to catch a porcupine, first look for his habitat. When you find the porcupine, circle him until he is in a

clearing. Then place a washtub over him. Now you will have time to sit down on the wash tub and contemplate what your next move should be.

God

580. I somehow can't believe that the Almighty exhausted himself when he invented the Gothic arch.

581. "My father taught me to believe in myself, and my mother taught me to believe in God."
"We believe in both of them at our house."

30, 86, 172, 242, 250, 255, 271, 280, 303, 373, 415, 502, 680, 712, 720, 743, 1018, 1033, 1034, 1036, 1080, 1290, 1382, 1418

Gold

582. Every morning I check the paper to see what the price of gold was the day before. I want to see if my mouth went up or down in value.

1267

Golf

583. Joe joined the country club just in case he needs a doctor on Wednesday afternoon.

584. Doctor: "You look awfully rundown. I suggest you lay off of golf for a while and get in a good day's work at the office."

585. A preacher chopped away in the sand trap. Finally he blasted the ball out of the trap (pause) into the trap on the other side of the green.
"Will one of you laymen please say something appropriate?"

586. The Pope made Arnold Palmer a monsignor so he could play in the ecumenical council golf tournament. Arnold came in second, right behind Rabbi Sam Snead.

587. Three members of a longtime foursome came in carrying the fourth. Joe had had a heart attack on the course, but he urged the others to play on.
"Wasn't he heavy, carrying him like that?"
"Yes, but the worst thing was laying him down and picking him up again between shots."

588. Jake Schwartz changed his name to John Black in order to join the fashionable non-Jewish country club. He took speech lessons to get rid of his accent. Despite all this, he was discovered anyway. You wonder how?

When he sliced the ball into the pond on the third hole, the waters parted.

589. Should Murphy tell Shapiro that he has his lost ball in his pocket?

590. A golfer lay beside the sand trap on the second hole.
"What's wrong?"
"Nothing wrong with me. My nine iron got overheated."

591. "Hey you can't do that. You're disqualified. You're driving from in front of the markers."
"Don't be silly. This is my third shot."

592. I have enough crises in my life without volunteering for eighteen more on my day off.

593. Jack couldn't get the women ahead of him to move by yelling "fore." Finally, when he yelled, "Three ninety-eight," they moved.

594. A golfer hooked the ball and injured a passing motorist. It was hit-and-run, but the police finally caught up with him.
"What are you going to do about it?"
"I think that next time I'll turn my left hand just a little," he said.

595. Golf is a form of work made expensive enough for a man to enjoy it.

267, 1158, 1170

Good News

596. This is the only country in the world where government argues over the size of the color TV set that a welfare family should get. This is the only country in the world where people going to get their unemployment check have a parking problem.

210, 610, 664

Government

597. Government big enough to give us everything we need must also be big enough to take everything we have.

598. Once the erosion of good government begins, it develops a momentum all its own.

599. Success in business is measured in inverse proportion to the amount of paper used. In government it is just the opposite.

600. "May I destroy these old government files?"

"Yes, provided you make a photocopy of each of them before you destroy them."

14, 192, 193, 454, 609, 652, 975, 1106, 1126, 1129, 1130, 1288, 1293, 1421

Governor

601. The Governor made a speech at the state prison. He began in his usual manner: "Fellow citizens . . ." A murmur of laughter went through the hall. Shaken, the Governor started over: "Fellow convicts . . ." The laughter increased.

"Oh, you know what I mean. I'm glad to see so many of you here today."

602. I don't know why they're criticizin' the Guvnor. He ain't done nuthin'.

603. Governor Frank Morrison of Nebraska said he still had some public support. When in the hospital, a group came to visit him. The spokesman of the group said that the staff had voted, and by a vote of 7-5, the staff wished him a speedy recovery.

706, 1004

Grandchild

604. The entire family was assembled for Thanksgiving dinner. All four children were there with spouses that they had recently married. Each couple was childless.

Before saying grace, Father said he would give $10,000 to the son or daughter who would present Mom and him with their first grandchild. Father bowed to pray. After the "Amen," he looked up to find nobody but Mom left at the table with him.

H

Handicap

605. At the mental institution, several men were chasing a naked woman. The man in back was carrying a bucket of sand.
   "Why the sand?"
   "He caught her yesterday. That is his handicap today."

Hanky-Panky

606. A man came into the barber shop, saw five people ahead of him, and he left. He came back the next day, saw six ahead of him, so he left. He came back the next day, found four ahead of him, so he left.
   Barber: "Follow that guy. See where he goes."
   "I know where he goes. He goes to your house."

607. "Who's this Ethel you talk about in your sleep?"
   "She's a horse I bet on."
   "Well, your horse called you today when you were out."

Hardware Store

608. A farmer coming into the hardware store asked for half of a six-foot stove pipe, cut lengthwise. The clerk in the store went to the man in the back room and told him, "Some nut out in front wants half of a six-foot stove pipe cut lengthwise." Then he looked around and there stood the customer. The clerk was a quick thinker. He said, "And this fine gentleman offered to take the other half."

Harvard

609. If you want to get into government service, go to Harvard, then turn left.

Heaven

610. My fortune cookie said, "I have good news and bad news. The good news is that you are going to go to heaven. The bad news is that they expect you there tomorrow."

611. A third-grader wrote, "I don't want to go to heaven. I want to be with my friends."

612. It was bound to happen sooner or later. St. Peter's High School was across from St. Joseph's Hospital. A woman, coming out of anesthesia heard music.
"Don't get excited, Mrs. Jackson. That's just St. Peter's Band."
"You mean . . ."
"No, I don't mean . . ."

613. Oley drove from Iron Mountain to Duluth. He had car trouble. He had the hood up and was hammering away and cursed as he hammered. His pastor came along.
"Oley, you'll never get to heaven that way."
"Aye doan vant to get to heaven. Aye vant to get to Duluth."

233, 620

Hermit

614. Three hermits went to the circus.
A year later one said, "That was a pretty white horse that that girl rode in the circus."
A year after that a second said, "That wasn't a white horse. It was a black horse."
A year after that, the third said, "I'm getting out of here. This constant wrangling is getting on my nerves."

Hills, The

615. There are so many curves in the mountains around Pigeon Forge that your headlights come in the back window and your tail-light pumps oil.

616. Dan'l Boone showed us how to make the hard stuff here in Kentucky, and he never came back to tell us to quit makin' it. In the Bible it speaks of wine made out of grapes. We don't like the taste of grapes in Kentucky. We use corn.

617. In the hills of Tennessee, a seven-course dinner is a possum and a six-pack.

618. At a Pigeon Forge wedding . . .

"Clem, your new son-in-law walked up the aisle like he had lead in his britches."

"He shore did."

619. Buford worked for a distillery in Kentucky. He fell into the vat. Several of his friends tried to save him, but Buford fought them off bravely. They cremated the body but couldn't get the fire out for three days.

620. We have a couple of maiden ladies on our road here in Pigeon Forge—the Henlitson sisters. They live next door to a retired minister who lost his dear wife, Emily, in a car accident three years ago. Every Tuesday night the Henlitson girls, friendly like, invite the reverend over for supper. After supper they go into the parlor and Alice sits on the piano stool and they have a good old fashioned hymn-sing for an hour or two.

Last week, the Reverend was leaning on the piano, arm on top, as he sang in his rich baritone voice. He accidentally knocked a box off the top of the piano onto the floor. The box opened. The Reverend looked, and couldn't believe what he saw. Prophylactics! He kept looking.

Alice, noticing the pastor's consternation, said, "Oh those, Reverend, yes, we found those among father's effects when he passed on a year ago. They were in his top dresser drawer in a box marked 'place on organ to prevent disease.' As you know, preacher, we don't have an organ so we put them on the piano. And it has been like a miracle from heaven. Ruth and me, neither one of us, has even had a cold since that time."

621. A man up in the hills south of Pigeon Forge traded his hog for a hound dog.

"Now, they won't be any meat in the house, Lem."

"Lissen here, old lady. Anybody knows you cain't run no fox with a hog."

622. A man came out of the hills to Knoxville for the first time. He was intrigued by the paved streets.

"No wonder they paved them. This is too hard to plow anyway."

623. A hill woman asked Sears for the price of their toilet paper. They told her to look on page 865.

"Iffen I had page 865, I wouldn't need no toilet paper."

624. A hillbilly was disgusted with the fact that his wife wouldn't talk to him. He took his gun, said he was going over the hill to shoot

himself. She heard a shot, then a voice that said, "Mirandy, fetch me another shell. I plumb missed myself the first time."

625. A Kentuckian was amazed at the uranium hunters.

"First there comes a feller with a goober counter looking for geraniums, then. . . ."

626. Most places, underwear comes packed in boxes of seven. You know—Monday, Tuesday, Wednesday . . .

Down in the hills we pack it in packages of twelve. You know—January, February, March . . .

627. The revenooer saw a boy in the yard in front of the hill cabin, west of Pigeon Forge.

"Where's your Paw?"

"Up to the still."

"Could you take me up there?"

"Sure could."

"I'll pay you a dollar to take me up there."

"Gimme the dollar."

"You'll get it when I get back."

"Mister, if you're going up to the still, you ain't a-comin' back."

628. Jeff and Sarah had twelve kids. When Doc Nelson came to deliver the twelfth one, he told Jeff, "Don't you think that's about enough?"

"Sure thing, Doc. Iffen we has one more, Ah's gwine to hang myself."

The next year Doc Nelson was back for the thirteenth time. "Don't I remember a promise you made a year ago, Jeff?"

"You sure does, Doc! Tha minute Ah sees that Ma was in a family way agin, Ah clumb up in that there apple tree and put a rope around my neck and around the limb of the apple tree. Ah was jist ready to jump off and then Ah thunk to myself, 'Jeff Wilkins, you might be hangin' tha wrong man.' "

Hippie

629. A hippie has hair like Tarzan, walks like Jane, and smells like Cheetah.

630. Two hippies were married in Pigeon Forge last week. They got married in the bathtub, thinking that would give their wedding more publicity. They had a double-ring ceremony.

631. Darwin said that his kinfolks were monkeys. He should know. They're his kin. Looking at some of the weirdos in rock bands, it looks like some people are headed right back in that direction again.

Hoax

632. A gagster passed around a petition in Washington to provide a pension for the widow of the Unknown Soldier. You'd be surprised how many signatures he got. A few even asked if she was still alive.

Hobby

633. Some people have a hobby of not working, but with this bum, it's a civic responsibility.

1284

Hockey

634. The goalie of the Detroit Red Wings took my son and me out to lunch. There we sat around the table. Father, son, and goalie host.

Home

635. A little hard work on the lawn in the spring will repay you (pause) with a lot of work later on.

636. Most accidents happen in the kitchen. The family has to eat them!

38, 184, 220, 385, 421, 422, 423, 431, 573, 581, 639, 686, 732, 754, 764, 879, 1080, 1161, 1383

Honeymoon

637. Bride sitting on hotel bed on her wedding night: "To think we're married. I just can't believe it!"

"You will if I ever get these blankety-blank shoelaces untied."

638. Sign on wedding car: The result of loose talk.

Hospitality

639. Hospitality is making people feel at home even though you wish they were.

Hotel

640. A New York couple, visiting Atlantic City for the first time, asked the hotel clerk for a room "facing the ocean . . . $20 or so."

They got a room facing the ocean for $20 plus tax. The room faced the Pacific Ocean.

641. I always register, "Mr. and Mistress" at hotels. You get better service that way. The other evening when I tipped the bellhop, he said, "Thank you, Senator."

642. If you ever hear the phrase, "send the s.o.b. the bedbug letter," it refers to the following classic story:

A traveling man stopped at a hotel in the county seat. He found bedbugs. He complained to the desk clerk, but the desk clerk said he should talk to the manager, who was out of town. When the traveling man got home, he wrote a barn-burning letter to the manager about the bedbugs.

He received a very cordial and apologetic reply. "This sort of thing has never happened here before. We have high standards of sanitation." The letter continued in that vein. But a little note had been clipped to the letter. It read: "Send this s.o.b. the bedbug letter."

149, 276, 418, 637, 759, 882, 886, 1092, 1277

Hunting

643. Two girls went deer hunting. One got a buck and the other got a buck and a half.

644. Two men were chased by a game warden. One stopped and the other ran. The game warden ran after the man who was trying to get away. He finally caught up with the culprit.

"Let's see your hunting license." The man produced a license.

"But why did you run if you have a hunting license?"

"My buddy didn't have a license."

645. Two hunters took along a little whiskey just in case of snake bite. They also brought a little box.

"What's in the box?"

"Two snakes."

646. The hunter shot, but the bird flew on.

"Fly, fly on you so-and-so. Fly with your gol-durned heart shot out if you want to."

647. I bought a shotgun that is almost new. A wealthy widow had it advertised in the paper. She said she used it only once.

414, 523, 571, 625, 1178

I

Ignorance

648. She was so dumb, we couldn't even get her to spell DDT.

649. He's the kind of person who when you say "Hello" to him, he's stuck for an answer.

650. Perhaps he is slow. He needs a bookmark when he reads the back of a cereal box.

940

Immigration

651. Chief Big Feather has given us good advice: Be careful with your immigration laws. Look at the trouble we Indians got into by being lax with ours.

Impersonating

652. If we don't get some money in our bank account soon, we'll be arrested for impersonating the government.

Impossible

653. When you get to the point where you think that nothing is impossible, try pushing toothpaste back into a tube or dribbling a football.

1343

Inadequate

654. Two cows looked at a sign: Pure Milk—Pasteurized—Homogenized—Vitamin D Added.
    One cow said to the other, "Makes one feel a bit inadequate, doesn't it?"

127

Inconsiderate

655. "The people upstairs are very inconsiderate. Last night, after midnight, they stomped and stomped on the floor."
   "Kept you awake, eh?"
   "No, as a matter of fact, it didn't. I was still practicing my tuba."

Indian

656. When the Indians saw Columbus land, they said, "There goes our neighborhood."

657. An Indian chief, inspecting a neighboring reservation, found that the restrooms were not wired for electricity. He wired them for electricity. He was the first person ever to wire a head for a reservation.

658. Paleface, he hear but don't listen, he look but don't see, he talk but don't say nothing.

659. Will Rogers was proud of his Indian blood. He said his ancestors didn't come over on the Mayflower—they were the welcoming committee when the Mayflower docked.

651, 855, 862, 1148

Indiana

660. Herb Shriner said he wasn't born in Indiana, but he moved there when he found out what a wonderful place it was.

661. Lincoln was born in Kentucky. Then the family moved to Indiana, where Indiana made Lincoln. He then went on to make Illinois.

662. "Son, when you go out into the world, don't ask people where they're from."
   "Why?"
   "If they come from Indiana they'll tell you about it for three hours. You were born and raised in Indiana and already know about it. And if people weren't born in Indiana, don't embarrass the folks."

Inflation

663. Inflation and recession have given us yet another problem. What kind of wine do you serve with nothing?

664. There's good news from the inflation front. Penny candy still only costs a quarter.

665. The dollar doesn't go as far as it used to, but what it lacks in distance it makes up in speed.

666. I have enough money for the rest of my life—at least unless I have to buy something.

Ingenuity

667. A man coming through a crowd with four hot dogs was getting nowhere by saying "Pardon me." Finally he yelled, "Watch out for the mustard!" He got a wide aisle to walk through.

668. Ivan pushed a wheelbarrow full of straw out of Strahorsky Communal Manufacturing every evening. Police knew he was stealing something, and inspected the straw microscopically, but found nothing that would permit them to indict Ivan. Finally they offered Ivan immunity from prosecution if he would tell them what it was that he was stealing.

"Wheelbarrows," Ivan replied.

669. "Why do you place water in the ashtrays?"

"To put out the cigarettes, and to keep the ashtrays from being stolen."

Injunction

670. "I thought I told you I didn't want you to continue seeing that young man. My dear, I gave you an injunction."

"Yes, I know. But my boyfriend took the case to a higher court. Mother told him it was all right."

In-Laws

671. "What are you doing with that dead horse in the middle of the street?"

"He was pulling my dray wagon and died. I sold him to the fertilizer company for $5. I'm waiting for the truck to come to pick him up."

"I'll give you ten bucks for that horse."

"Brother, you just bought yourself a horse."

"I can't use him here. Deliver him to 1585 Osage Trail."

"You just paid for a horse. You didn't pay for freight. That will cost you another ten spot."

"Here's your twenty bucks."

Arriving at 1585 Osage Trail: "Now take him up to the third floor, Apartment B, and put him in the bathtub."

"That'll be another $10 for porter charges."

"Here's your $10."

"But why in the world do you want a dead horse in the bathtub?"

"You'd have to know my brother-in-law. They come over every Saturday night to play bridge. He's such a smart s.o.b. He asks things like, 'George, how many trees are there in the national forests?' How do I know? Then he rattles off, '10,873,793,172.' His wife beams on account of what a smart man she married. My wife gives me a dirty look that says, 'You dumb cluck!'

Then he asks, 'George, how many stars are there in the Milky Way constellation?' Of course I don't know that, so we get a repeat of the act. His wife smirks and my wife scowls.

This Saturday night it's going to be different. After he mouths off a couple of times like that, and has a few beers, he'll have to go to the bathroom. He'll come out running, yelling, 'George, what in the world is that you have in the bathtub?' That's when I get even, finally! I'll smile and say, 'You dingbat, that's a dead horse.' "

672. Mother-in-law to new groom: "Never forget; you weren't our first choice."

673. "Do you mean to say that your mother tried to keep you from marrying me?"

"Yes."

"Good Lord, how I've wronged that woman all these years!"

674. We went to Yellowstone. Old Faithful and my mother-in-law were both spouting off at the same time.

Inspector

675. A highway inspector noted for his fault-finding inspected a newly completed portion of road. The crown was not high enough. The shoulder was too steep. The ditches were not deep enough.

The contractor took it as long as he could stand it, and then said sarcastically, "How is she for length?"

657, 668, 880, 913, 1132

Insurance

676. "How much life insurance do you have?"

"$5,000."

"Don't expect to be dead long, do you?"

677. Insurance salesman: "If you look as good on the inside as you do on the outside, I believe I can get you some more life insurance."

678. An insurance salesman stuck his head into the sales manager's office door and said, "You don't want to buy any insurance, do you?"

"No!"

Pause.

"Young man, come back here. Whoever taught you how to sell? 'Don't want to buy any insurance, do you?' " The sales manager lectured him on salesmanship, stressing that every customer's needs are different.

"What you lack is confidence. Get out your application blanks. I'll buy some of your insurance to give you confidence."

The application was filled out. "Now remember what I told you. Every customer is different. You use different approaches for each customer."

"I do that."

"What do you mean, you do that?"

"This is my approach for sales managers, and it works almost every time."

Inventor

679. We have a fellow in Pigeon Forge who is a whiz at inventions. He invented a device that permits people to see through a solid wall. He calls it a window.

410, 580

Irish

680. They asked Patrick Hooley to run for alderman in South Minneapolis. "You must be out of your mind. A Roman Catholic among all these Norwegian Lutherans?" But they persisted, so Pat ran and won. Then he won reelection. Then his friends suggested that he run for mayor. Once again Pat resisted, but his friends insisted. Pat ran and won. The Reverend Swenson of St. Lutefisk Lutheran Church asked the Mayor to come over to say a few words during the intermission of the Christmas concert.

"Only in America could this happen. A Roman Catholic among all you Norwegian Lutherans and you elect me alderman and then mayor. I don't mind telling you that I am flattered when the children in the playgrounds say, 'Good morning, Your Honor.' I am delighted when the ladies in the shops say, 'Good afternoon, Your Honor.' I am thrilled through and through when the gentlemen at meetings in the evening say, 'Good evening, Your Honor.' But Pastor Swenson, tonight you carried the approbation a bit too far when you had your choir sing, 'Hooley, Hooley, Hooley, Lord God Almighty' before you introduced me."

681. "She married an Irishman."

"Oh, really?"

"No, O'Riley."

682. "Pat, what's this I hear about ye joinin' up with the Commies? Be ye daft, man?"

"It's the truth, Mike. I signed up last week. The doctor told me I have only one month to live. Better that one of those bloody Communists dies than a good Irishman."

683. Once upon a time there were two Irish people. Now there are millions of them.

684. Is this a private fight, or can anyone join in?

541

Irony

685. First we heat tea to make it hot and then we put ice cubes in it to make it cold. Then we add sugar to make it sweet and lemon to make it sour. Then we say, "Here's to you!" and we drink it ourselves. Confusing, isn't it?

686. Why do people complain when they get short weight on the butcher's scale, and then go home to set their bathroom scale wrong?

I.R.S.

687. A South Carolina farmer had a record of practical jokes. He raises goats and when one of the goats has a bellyache, he gives it whiskey. When he files his 1040 tax form, he lists, "whiskey for the kids." That always gets a rise out of the I.R.S. but he always wins.

688. You've heard that you can't get something for nothing. Send nothing to the I.R.S. and you'll get something.

689. "I've been pestered with threatening letters and I want you folks here in the Post Office to do something about it."

"Do you have any idea who is sending you these threatening letters?"

"I sure do. It's those damn tax people! I.R.S., they calls themselves."

690. I.R.S. installs special phones at tax time for people who like to listen to busy signals.

691. If the earth is getting smaller all the time, like everybody says, why is it that the I.R.S.'s tax bills get bigger every year?

692. I just figured out why we have deficits. We work five days per week and government spends money and the I.R.S. collects money seven days per week.

J

Jail

693. "Sam, how come you're in jail?"
"Throwing rocks out of my neighbor's yard into mine."
"What's wrong with that?"
"They were Plymouth Rocks."

694. We're getting a better class of people in our jails today.

12, 217, 501, 702

Jealousy

695. Paint me with diamond earrings, a diamond necklace, emerald bracelets. My husband is running around with some young chick. If I die, I want her to go nuts looking for the jewelry.

Judge

696. Judge Weeks spotted a man in his courtroom who was wearing a hat. Disturbed by this lack of courtroom decorum, the judge ordered the man ejected from the courtroom.
"We will now hear the case of George Rogje."
"But, Your Honor, that is the man that you just ordered ejected from the courtroom."
(P.S. They still haven't found George.)

697. Judge: "I commend you two careless drivers for having run into each other instead of some innocent motorist or pedestrian. If this sort of thing can be encouraged, it may prove to be the solution to a very serious problem in this city."

698. Judge: "So you were gambling. Is that correct?"
Defendant: "Yes, but we weren't playing for money, Your Honor."
Judge: "What were you playing for?"
Defendant: "Chips."

Judge: "That's the same as money. $25 fine. Next case."

The defendant paid with twenty-five chips.

699. It was a long and brutal cross-examination.

Judge: "Are you or are you not sure that this man stole your car on the night of November 10?"

"Your Honor, after that cross-examination, I'm not even sure that I ever owned a car."

700. Judge: "Did you see the shot fired?"

"No, but I heard it."

"Insufficient evidence. Step down."

Joe didn't like this kind of justice so on the way out of the court, he laughed derisively.

Judge: "Don't you know that I could fine you for contempt of court for laughing that way?"

"Did you see me laugh?"

No, but I heard you."

"Insufficient evidence, Your Honor," and Joe walked out of the courtroom.

701. Judge: "Have you ever earned an honest dollar?"

"Oh yes, Your Honor. I voted for you in the last election."

702. Two judges came to court on traffic charges, only to find no judge presiding. They decided to try each other. One fined the other $25 for speeding.

The second judge threw the other into jail for 30 days on the same charge of speeding. "This is the second case of this kind that has come to the attention of this court this morning," he said.

703. Judge: "The defendant's right to lie was infringed upon. Case dismissed."

704. "I'm sorry, but I didn't hear your answer."

"What part of it didn't you hear? I'll repeat it."

705. "What sentence did you get?"

"Ten dollars per word."

"Ten dollars per word?"

"Yes. I talked back to the judge."

706. "It seems to me that you have appeared before me in this court a dozen times in the last twenty years."

"I can't help it, Your Honor, that you have so little talent that the Governor doesn't promote you to a higher court."

707. There is something this court should know. An hour ago, the plaintiff gave me $1,000 as a present. Right after that, the defendant

gave me $1,500. I am now going to give the defendant back $500 and then we will try this case on its merits.

708. Judge: "I am sentencing you to three years in prison because you did not rid your warehouse of rats."

"But I thought rats were an endangered species."

"Only in Washington, DC."

66, 193, 306, 370, 413, 540

Jury

709. A woman was questioned about jury duty. She pleaded to be excused because she did not believe in capital punishment.

"But this is merely a case where a wife is suing her husband because she gave him $1,000 to put down on a fur coat and he lost the money at the race track."

"I've changed my mind. I'll serve. I could be wrong about capital punishment."

Juvenile Delinquency

710. Do you remember when it was considered juvenile delinquency for a boy to owe 12 cents on an overdue library book? Do you remember when that's about all the juvenile delinquency we had?

K

Kansas

711. A Kansas farmer bought some windstorm insurance. Every time the radio told of storm warnings, he dived for his storm cellar. Sixty-seven times he came out and there was the house and barn. On the sixty-eighth trip out, the house was destroyed and the barn was half gone.

"Now, that's more like it!"

712. It's all in the way you say it . . .

You can say, "Good bye, God. I'm going to Kansas." Or you can say, "Good! By God, I'm going to Kansas."

L

Lawn

713. "Thank goodness, my crab grass problem is finally solved."
"How did you solve it?"
"The dandelions are crowding out the crab grass."

116, 447, 555, 635, 911, 1305, 1306

Lawsuit

714. The court wouldn't have awarded anything at all if I hadn't had the presence of mind to give my wife a kick in the face as our car was rolling over.

66

Lawyer

715. Attorney Maddik spent the whole night breaking down the widow's will.

716. A person accused of a crime needs a lawyer (pause) especially if the person is guilty.

717. "They are about to put me in the electric chair. What do I do now? You're my lawyer. I need advice!"
"Refuse to sit down."

12, 860, 1088

Leadership

718. Leadership is the art of getting somebody else to do something you want done because that person wants to do it.

Legislature

719. Louisiana's John John III introduced a bill that requires all shopping centers to have rest rooms. Folks down in the bayou country call this bill the John John John Bill.

Liberals

720. Liberals tell us they are doing the work of the Lord, but did you ever try to get one on the phone before 9:30 a.m.? Or after 4:30 p.m.?

Library

721. Jimmy came to the library's check-in counter with a well-worn book. The librarian said, "This is rather technical, isn't it?"
   "It was that way when I took it out."

209, 710

Life

722. "Life is like a fountain."
   "Why is that?"
   "Okay, so life is not like a fountain."

162, 278, 320, 379, 387, 592, 666, 752, 786, 853, 923, 943, 959, 1076, 1252, 1397

Listen

723. You can learn more by listening than by talking, but it's not nearly as much fun.

255, 363, 467, 489, 658, 959, 1063, 1307, 1389

Loan Company

724. I borrowed $50 from my Super Friendly Loan Company. I've paid them back $80, and when I pay the remaining $89, I'll be all paid up.

Lodge

725. "Does this lodge have any death benefits?"
   "Sure does. When you die, you won't need to pay dues anymore."
726. "I'm a Mason."
   "Glad to know you. I use your jars."

Lucidity

727. Public servants are known for their lucidity. Here's a question asked of Senator Teddy Kennedy, and his answer.

"Senator, how would you cope with the Soviet Union?"

"Well, I think we need a foreign policy which is tied to our national policy and security interests which is tied to our national policy and security interests which are tied to intelligent interests for the U.S. that are tied to energy interests, which are tied to a sound economy here in the U.S. and an energy policy that is going to free us from heavy dependence on Persian Gulf countries and OPEC, which is strongly, which has a down side to it in terms of disincentives to the Soviet Union for actions which are contrary to the ah, uh, to uh, a standard of both international behavior and also has disincentives for the USSR."

Huh?

Lutheran

728. Best seller: *I Was a Teenage Roman Catholic*, by Martin Luther.

729. A Lutheran preacher wore a clerical collar in a Catholic neighborhood.

"That's the Lutheran father at St. Paul's."

"He ain't a father. He's got three kids."

680, 830, 1135, 1140

M

Magazine

730. Doctor: "People read the *Reader's Digest* and get diseases I've never even heard of."

Maiden Lady

731. A robber searched the maiden lady for twenty minutes but found nothing.
   "Haven't you got any money?"
   "No, but keep on searching. I'll write you a check."

732. Millie had a tomcat that she always kept in the house. Then Millie went on a vacation and discovered the male sex. When she got home, she let her tomcat out of the house occasionally.

733. A little old lady spent days working on a pair of men's pajamas, which she contributed to the Red Cross.
   "I made these myself," she said proudly. The Red Cross lady looked at the pajamas admiringly, then noted that there was no opening in the front of the pants. When she explained the error, the dear old lady's face fell.
   "Couldn't you give them to a bachelor?"

734. Maiden lady: "I'm too young for Medicare and too old for men to care."

493, 620

Make Ends Meet

735. About the time that we get to the point that we make ends meet, the politicians move the ends for us.

736. When you watch TV, you watch somebody else make a lot of money at their profession. You make nothing that contributes to making ends meet.

93

Marines

737. Sign in hieroglyphics on the wall of Montezuma's tomb: Marines note: No Singing Allowed.

738. A Marine has loyalty to his country and his branch of service that is akin to a Virginian's loyalty to Robert E. Lee.

739. "What are you doing?"
   "Procrastinating."
   "Good. Just so you keep busy. Remember the esprit de corps the Marines have."

740. We haven't heard from John since the enemy got him and put him in one of their constipation camps.

23, 49

Markets

741. From college, a daughter wrote her father: "In Philosophy I, four boys like me. In French, two boys like me. In Geology, three boys like me. That's a total of nine; up three from last semester."

742. Bulls and bears make money, but hogs go broke.

1004

Marriage

743. Thank the good Lord he permitted Charley and Erma to get married. That way there will only be two miserable people instead of four.

744. She has something that will knock your eyes out. A husband!

745. When Joseph H. Choate was asked at a dinner party, "If you couldn't be yourself, who would you rather be?"
   He said, "Mrs. Choate's *second* husband!"

746. "Dear Mrs. Blank: Johnny is a bright boy but he spends all his time with the girls. I'm trying to think of some way to cure him. Signed, Johnny's teacher."
   "Dear Teacher: If you find some way to cure him, please let me know. I'm having the same trouble with his father. Signed, Mrs. Blank."

747. My wife is so fussy that when I get up to get a midnight snack, I return to find the bed made.

748. I walked past the cemetery. A man sat on a grave sobbing, "Why did he have to die? Why did he have to die?"

I offered my condolences in his hour of grief. "Was it your father?"

"No, it wasn't my father."

"Your son then?"

"No, it wasn't my son. Oh, why did he have to die?"

"A brother perhaps?"

"No, it wasn't my brother."

"Then who was it?"

"My wife's first husband. Oh, why did he have to die?"

749. "St. Peter, is my husband here? His name is Smith."

"We have a lot of Smiths here. Could you be more specific?"

"Joe Smith."

"We have a lot of Joe Smiths too. Is there any other identification?"

"Well, when he died, he said that if I was ever unfaithful to him, he would turn over in his grave."

"Oh, you mean Pinwheel Smith. Yes, he's here!"

750. "When should you tell your wife you love her?"

"Before the other guy does."

751. "I was a fool to ever have married you."

"I guess you were, but I was so in love with you that I didn't notice."

752. "Married life is great. I'm married to a woman who can't tell a lie."

"You lucky devil. My wife can tell a lie the minute it is out of my mouth."

753. Mary bought herself a new pair of stretch pants.

"How do you like them, dear?"

"Makes your feet look big too."

754. "I asked you to mail this letter a month ago. I just found it in your coat pocket."

"Oh, yes. That's the coat I left at home so you could sew a button on it, isn't it?"

755. "You look all dragged out. What happened to you?"

"Well, I was coming home at five o'clock this morning. I started to get undressed when my wife said, 'You're getting up a little early, aren't you?' To prevent an argument, I just got dressed again."

756. Hubby wanted to chop off the dog's tail. He didn't want to leave any sign around the house that his mother-in-law was welcome.

757. "I finally got two tickets for the show."

"Good, I'll start dressing."

"Good idea. The show is tomorrow night."

758. My wife has Gimbels well on the way to economic recovery, and now she's starting on Marshall Fields.

759. I thought I had brought my briefcase along. My wife insisted that I had left it at the hotel. So, not distrusting my wife, I went back to the hotel and found it. In the ladies' restroom!

760. George is the most generous husband that ever lived. He gives me everything that credit cards will buy.

761. The only two who can live as cheaply as one are a flea and a dog.

762. Rubber heel ad: I'm in love with America's #1 Heel!

Under this was scrawled, "Sorry, Sis, you're too late. I married him."

763. "How's your wife?"

"Compared to what?"

764. When I got home last evening, my wife greeted me with a big kiss. She had a wonderful supper and wouldn't allow me to help her with the dishes. She told me to go into the living room and read the paper. How do *you* like the new dress she bought?

765. John is Mr. Fixit. The other night he fixed our cuckoo clock. Now the cuckoo backs out, scratches its head, and asks what time it is.

766. Nobody can cook like Mabel can cook, but they came close to it in the Army.

767. We've got four kids. That's not a record, but it's a darn good average.

768. I took my wife to the convention. You know how it is, you take things along you don't need.

769. Let's give practical gifts to each other this Christmas. Like neckties and fur coats.

770. I call my wife Shasta. Shasta have this. Shasta have that.

771. Hubby stepped on the scale. The little card read: "You are intelligent, have a magnetic personality, strength of character; you are a leader of men, you are intelligent and handsome and attracted by the opposite sex."

His wife read the card, then said, "The weight's wrong too."

772. "Goodbye, mother of five."

"Goodbye, father of three."

773. Jack was married twice. Both wives died. He asked to be buried between Millie and Tillie, but he said, "Tilt me a little toward Tillie."

774. "Has your husband taken the prescription I gave him? A tablet before each meal and a little whiskey afterward?"

"Doctor, he's two weeks behind on the tablets and three weeks ahead on the whiskey."

775. "My wife doesn't know what she wants."
   "You're lucky. Mine does."

776. Monday you liked beans. Tuesday you liked beans. Wednesday you liked beans. Now all of a sudden on Thursday, you don't like beans. Make up your mind!

777. "Wake up, Tom. There's a burglar going through your pants pockets."
   "Leave me out of this. You two fight it out by yourselves."

778. "Bill kisses Mabel every morning. Why don't you do that?"
   "Why, I hardly know Mabel."

779. My wife is wearing "Evening in Paris." I'm wearing "Afternoon at the Stockyards."

780. "I'll bet if I were married, I'd be the boss and I would tell my wife where to head in at."
   "Yeah, and I suppose when you come to a railroad track, you honk and the train just jumps out of the way."

781. The early part of our marriage went really fine, and then on the way out of the church . . .

782. "I have half a mind to get married."
   "That's all you need, brother. That's all you need!"

783. Marry for money and suffer in comfort.

784. I could only afford half a wife and with my luck, I got the half that eats.

785. Model husband. I looked up the word "model" and the dictionary says it is a cheap imitation of the real thing.

786. My wife and I have a perfect understanding. I don't try to run her life, and I don't try to run mine either.

787. "Your husband is lying unconscious in the hallway!"
   "Goody, goody. My fur coat has come!"

788. "How dare you burp before my wife?"
   "I didn't know it was her turn."

789. "I'm ready now."
   "Take your time. I have to shave again."

790. How do you expect me to remember your birthday, when on every birthday you look younger than on the birthday before?

791. Do you know that 50 percent of all married people are women?

792. Ever since the Smiths bought that waterbed, they seem to be drifting apart.

793. My wife lets me go out with the boys once a week. The Boy Scouts that is.

794. She believes in law and order. She lays down the law and he obeys the orders.

795. It was a pleasure trip. I took my wife over to her mother's house.

796. Mrs. Sherwood said her husband didn't make the living for the family, but he made the living worthwhile.

158, 176, 198, 234, 261, 346, 351, 353, 394, 442, 604, 630, 671, 673, 681, 894, 1045, 1068, 1076, 1260, 1311, 1363, 1412. Also see Husband, Wife, Father, Mother.

Martini

797. What's wrong with the three-martini lunch? How else can one get an eyeful, an earful, a stomach-full and a snoot-full all at one setting?

883

Mass Transit

798. If you're waiting for a bus, it never comes. If you're driving your car, the bus is always right there in front of you.

799. A Quaker ran for the bus. He thought he was gaining on it, but in a fit of meanness, the bus driver pulled away just as the man got alongside the bus. Mud splashed on the man.
    Quaker: "May his soul find peace (pause), and the sooner the better."

800. When the bus company placed signs on its buses that read: How far away did you have to park today? Perkins put a bumper sticker on his car that read: How far did you have to walk to the bus today? Then he deliberately plunked himself in front of, or alongside of, the city's buses.

960, 1328

Maternity

801. "How far apart are your wife's labor pains?"
    "They're all in the same place."

802. Registering at maternity ward desk: "Honey, are you sure you want to go through with this?"

MC

803. I know that our speaker is a gentleman. Just a few moments ago I saw him come out of a door that says so.

804. There are two kinds of speakers: (1) those that need no introduction, and (2) those who don't deserve an introduction. Fortunately, our speaker is in the first category.

805. William Allen White was scheduled to speak. The MC showed White the lengthy introduction. White waved it aside with, "Just tell 'em I'm here and I'll make a speech."

806. I'll not lie about you if you promise not to tell the truth about me.

807. Our speaker is the MFWIC—Main Fellow What's in Charge of this here organization.

808. We will now break for lunch. That is an old custom that we started way back during the Coolidge administration.

809. Our speaker is a famous author. He has written such best sellers as
Let Leaking Faucets Leak, Squeaking Floors Have a Charm All Their Own, House Painting Can Be Fun, But I Don't See How, and *If at First You Don't Succeed, Give Up.*

810. Our speaker has an IQ roughly triple his belt size.

811. We planned to present a speaker who has not yet arrived. He went to confession last Tuesday and hasn't come out yet. If he gets here, he should have a very interesting story to tell.

812. The Program Committee voted not to have a program tonight. Now we will hear from . . .

813. Our speaker is such a great guy that even the undertaker is going to hate to see him go.

814. Our speaker is an ex-young newspaper man.

815. Our speaker is also a composer. He wrote the popular song, "When They Operated on Father, They Opened Mother's Male."

816. Considering all the great things our speaker has accomplished in his (her) short lifetime, he (she) should be at least 138 years old.

817. We will now hear from the quartet. I sang in a quartet back home. We called ourselves the "Fish Market Four." We had a first and second tuna, a barracuda, and a bass.

818. Our head table needs no introduction, they already know each other.

Medical Science

819. It is true that medical science still has no cure for the common cold, but research has developed several miracle drugs which, if taken under a doctor's strict supervision, will keep the cold from getting any worse.

820. When they find a cure for a disease, why is it that the scientists take all the credit? The white mice did all the work!

1018, 1334, 1335

Memory

821. "I can remember everything that happened in my boyhood, whether it happened or not." Mark Twain.

Men

822. "If you hold a dog, he licks your hands and doesn't bite you. That's the main difference between a man and a dog." Mark Twain.

823. I hate to go to the beach. Have you ever tried to hold your stomach in for six hours?

824. I require twice as much money as I used to to live beyond my means.

825. I used to be a boxer. I boxed oranges, grapefruit, grapes, and apples.

826. A man who had lost his sexual vigor took some youth pills. Then he turned up missing. His wife thought maybe he was with the young widow down the street. Instead he was sitting on the curb, crying, "I missed my school bus."

827. They sent his picture to "Ripley's Believe It or Not," but Ripley sent it back. He couldn't believe it either.

828. When two men compared notes, they found that they were husbands-in-law.

104, 105, 121, 122, 123, 124, 202, 261, 306, 334, 338, 418, 429, 431, 439, 451, 475, 537, 550, 595, 605, 608, 621, 628, 644, 667, 670, 734, 771, 880, 896, 935, 983, 1037, 1105, 1118, 1143, 1371, 1387, 1397, 1398, 1409, 1418

Methodist

829. "You look anemic."
   "No, I'm Methodist."

830. "When we get to heaven, us Methodists are going to have front-row seats."

"Why is that, Daddy?"

"Because the Lutherans will be out front arguing with each other and the Catholics will be downstairs playing Bingo."

128, 1101, 1135

Mexican

831. An American physics professor was crossing the Mexican border. "What business are you in, Señor?"

"Physics."

There were language problems. After hurried conference:

"Retail or wholesale?"

832. "But I doan want to be transferred to Tampico. All Tampico has isa baseball players an prostitutes."

"Watch what you say, Señor! My mother, she come from Tampico."

"Your mother, she come from Tampico? How nice! Doesa she play infield or outfield?"

Michigan

833. Michigan, our inland empire of the unsalted seas!

Money

834. If money gets any tighter, it will be as hard to get into debt as it is to get out of it.

835. Some people have trouble with money, but there are a lot more people who have trouble without it.

836. A dollar is pretty good bait!

837. Money isn't everything, but if you're in business, it's way ahead of whatever is in second place.

94, 161, 167, 197, 282, 322, 326, 383, 446, 472, 510, 567, 652, 666, 692, 698, 709, 731, 736, 742, 783, 824, 855, 1017, 1050, 1051, 1082, 1122, 1215, 1301, 1377

Motel

838. The Smiths, traveling with their dog, inquired at the motel whether the dog would be permitted in their room.

The desk clerk answered, "I've been in this business thirty years. I have never had to call the police to eject a disorderly dog. I have never had a dog set fire to the bed clothes with a cigarette. I have never found one of my towels in a dog's suitcase. Certainly, your dog is welcome. And if he will vouch for you, you can come in too."

149, 357, 1206

Museum

839. In the museum they showed us two skulls of Marco Polo. One was when he was a boy.

209

N

Natural Ingredients

840. Label on box of rat poison: Contains only natural ingredients.

Navy

841. Bronze plaque on battleship: "Here is where Admiral Bledsoe fell."

Sailor: "I'm not surprised. I darn near tripped over it myself."

842. The U.S.S. *Seadragon* cruised under the North Pole and then surfaced long enough to let the crew stretch and play a three-inning game of baseball. The North Pole was home plate. First base was in the Eastern Hemisphere. Third base was in the Western Hemisphere. The catcher hit a pop fly that the third baseman caught the next day.

843. In the American Revolution, a sailor in the crow's nest sighted the British. The ships, came together as cannons fired. The ships came so close together that there was rifle fire. The British admiral told John Paul Jones to surrender. John Paul Jones said, "I have not yet begun to fight."

The sailor in the crow's nest, who had been dodging rifle and cannon fire, said, "There's one in every crowd who hasn't gotten the message."

844. "The fleet's in. Better lock up your girls."

"No need to worry. My girls have it up here (pointing to head)."

"I don't care where they've got it. The sailors on these ships will find it."

845. "Am I the first girl you ever kissed?"

Sailor: "Come to think of it, your face is familiar."

846. Joe took a bottle of wine on every date. He wanted a little port in every girl.

310, 1237, 1238

New England

847. A New Englander repaired a chimney. Four months later, he still hadn't sent a bill.

"Folks around here are in no hurry to pay bills, so why should I be in a hurry to send them out?"

848. The New Englander was asked if she was going to take a vacation. She said she was already there.

Newlyweds

849. New bride: "Joe said he was going out to shoot craps. I don't know how to prepare craps, Mother. Do you have a recipe?"

Newspaper

850. Hydrogen doesn't explode in a nuclear plant, but it is highly volatile in the press.

851. When the Times Building was torn down in New York City, the cornerstone, dated 1906, was opened. The newspaper in the cornerstone carried stories about:
1. Trouble in the Far East
2. Trouble in Africa
3. Trouble in Panama
4. Police fighting organized crime
5. Cigarettes being bad for the health
So what else is new?

852. Our newspaper was late this week because of a corn field. It seems that the corn fermented, which got the pressman into trouble, and that delayed the paper.

853. News item: "Mrs. Clark was overcome by gas fumes while bathing. She owes her life to the watchfulness of her neighbor, Sheldon Shears, who lives across the alley."

854. "Do you have a newspaper here in the barber shop?"
"No, just the New York Times."

147, 582, 647, 764, 814, 860, 945, 1143, 1334

New York

855. We paid $24 for Manhattan, but the Battery was not included—it cost $12 extra. If the Indians had invested that $36 at 6 percent compounded interest. I would now be able to buy the world and have money left over.

856. Three ways to gamble in New York . . .
   1. Off-track betting
   2. State lottery
   3. Walk in Central Park

63, 80, 314, 851, 854, 1260

Nurse

857. A nurse saw a report that read, "Shot in lumbar region." She changed it to read, "Shot in the woods."

858. Doctor: "Have you kept a chart on his progress?"
   Nurse: "No, but I can show you my diary."

859. As a pigeon flew over the mental hospital grounds, it left a deposit on one of the park benches. A nurse said she would go after some toilet paper.

   "And they think we're nuts. Why, by the time she gets back, that pigeon will be long gone."

460

O

Obituary

860. A man's obituary appeared in the daily paper. He called his lawyer to sue the newspaper.
    Lawyer: Where are you calling from?

147, 1069

Oil

861. We're not short of oil. Our dipstick's just too short.

862. Oil was first discovered by an Indian. He saw this black stuff coming out of the ground, so he took off his shirt and soaked the shirt in the black stuff. When the Indian arrived back at his teepee, he wrung the shirt out in a pot. Hence the word "potroleum," which palefaces have since corrupted into "petroleum." The oil didn't do the shirt any good either. This Indian was the first man to lose his shirt in the oil business.

172, 391, 615

Oldsters

863. I still chase women, but only downhill.

864. I don't sleep in the same room with my teeth anymore.

865. When Mozart was my age, he had been dead for seventeen years. That's a sobering thought. You knew he was dead, didn't you? If you didn't, I'm the bearer of sad tidings.

866. "Do you have any Lifebuoy?"
    "Honey, you just set the pace."

867. My first job was parking covered wagons.

868. I'm so old that I remember when comic books cost a dime and gum didn't.

869. When you get older, you wait until you drop something before bending down to tie your shoelaces.

870. "Doc, I'd like to have you lower my sex drive."
   "But you're 85 years old, Clate. It's all in your head."
   "I know. That's why I want it lowered."

871. When you get older, you feel your toothbrush in the morning. If it's wet, you know you have already brushed your teeth.

872. I looked down to find that I was wearing one black and one brown shoe. I didn't remember ever buying a pair of shoes like that. When I got home, I found I had another pair just like that in the closet.

873. You're getting older when you talk more with your druggist than you do with your bartender.

874. I'm so old I can remember when TV sets ran on whale oil.

875. I'm so old that I really do fool Mother Nature.

876. When Betsy Ross showed me her flag, I said, "Looks a little busy to me, but run 'er up on a flagpole. If somebody salutes your flag, you know you have a winner."

877. I am a bionic geriatric.

878. I'm so old that when a girl says "no," I say, "Thank you!"

879. When I am faced with temptation, I choose the alternative that gets me home by 8:30.

880. A man is getting old when he inspects the food instead of the waitresses.

881. I'm in my second childhood. I have braces on my false teeth.

882. She agreed to go up to the hotel room with me, but said, "Bring a bottle." I brought a bottle of (pause) Geritol.

883. He's so old he orders prunes instead of olives for his martinis.

884. I remember when there were other things besides the PTA behind the school.

885. I worked for Stanley Steamer and got fired because I forgot to bring matches.

886. The other night some fellows took me downstairs in the hotel to the disco. I had never been in one of those dens of iniquity before. The wiggling and squirming of those young folks just made me tired looking at them. Everything moved but their bowels. If a dog would have done that, they would have given him worm medicine.

887. When I was young I could pick up my handkerchief with my teeth. Now I pick up teeth with my handkerchief.

888. When a good-looking young woman walks by, my pacemaker makes the garage doors go up.

889. You are old if you remember:
Dirty theatres that showed clean films
Bathing suits that wore out at the knee
When the problems with pot were limited to finding the darned thing under the bed.

890. I lost my bridge in the River Kwai.

891. I'm the Rock Hudson of the Geritol set.

16, 130, 280, 345, 404, 428, 733, 734, 814, 929

Opera

892. Robert Donat was a guest of honor at an opera box party given by a prominent member of society. To Donat's increasing irritation, the hostess talked during the performance. Toward the end of the opera, she leaned over to Donat and said, "Oh my dear Mr. Donat, would you be our guest tomorrow night too? The opera will be *Tosca*."

Donat replied,"I would be delighted. I have never heard of you in *Tosca*."

Opportunity

893. Opportunity is a dog in a lot full of Christmas trees.

Optimist

894. They're both 83, and they got married. They're looking for a house near a school. Now, that's what I call optimism.

895. An optimist is a person who will attempt to raise roses, vegetables, chickens, two cocker spaniels, and three boys at one and the same time. Can't be done!

896. An incurable optimist always said, "Things could be worse."
One day he was told of a man who had caught his wife with another man. Both wife and lover were shot.

"Could have been worse."

"What do you mean by that? What could be worse than a double murder?"

"It could have been the day before. Then he would have shot me."

897. Optimism is what makes a tea kettle sing when it is in hot water up to its neck.

898. An optimist thinks that all women are sexy. A pessimist just hopes they are.

916, 920, 1264

Optometrist

899. A young optometrist just out of school asked an elderly optometrist, "We learned everything in school except what to charge. What do you charge for glasses?"

"I look the patient straight in the eye and say, 'That will be $35.' If the patient doesn't flinch, I add 'for the frames.' Then I say, 'The lenses will cost another $35.' If the patient doesn't flinch this time either, I add, 'per lens.' "

Organization

900. A Texan, who was proficient with a whip, was asked to flick a hornets nest.

"Sorry, pardner. A fly is a fly, but a hornets' nest is an organization."

Orient

901. A visitor from the U.S. asked a Hong Kong policeman for directions to Wong Lee, the famous tailor. He was told to look up the number in the white pages.

902. One billion Chinese, and they still say their favorite sport is ping-pong.

903. Message in fortune cookie: "Please disregard message in previous cookie."

1380, 1391

Outhouse

904. The l'Enfance outhouse perched precariously on the edge of the bayou. On the way to school, little Pierre couldn't resist the temptation. He pushed the l'Enfance outhouse into the bayou.

After school Daddy l'Enfance lined up his boys. "Which one of you pushed the outhouse into the bayou?"

Pierre: "Daddy, I cannot tell a lie. I pushed the outhouse into the bayou."

Daddy gave little Pierre the thrashing of his young life.

"But Daddy, when George Washington told his Daddy that he had chopped down the cherry tree, his Daddy didn't whup him."

"Yes, but George Washington's Daddy wasn't up in that cherry tree either."

P

Panhandler

905. Panhandler: "Mister, would you give me five dollars for a cup of coffee?"

"Five dollars for a cup of coffee? Man, are you out of your mind?"

"OK, so don't give me five dollars for a cup of coffee then, but don't tell me how to run my business."

Parachute

906. I don't want to join the paratroopers. You have to do everything right the first time.

907. The woman whose parachute didn't open jumped to conclusions.

1264

Parody

908. Revisions of famous quotes:

"Surrender, hell! We have just begun to negotiate."

"Millions for defense, but not one cent for victory."

"50-40 or a reasonable compromise."

"Damn the torpedoes, we're unilaterally disarmed."

Party

909. The Hendersons planned a gala party for twenty guests. Matty had everything perfectly planned. But just before the party, she came into the kitchen to find the cat eating the salmon mousse. She kicked the cat out of the door and smoothed over the mousse with a knife. The party went off just perfectly. As the Hendersons cleaned up after the guests had departed, Matty took the garbage out and found the cat dead on the back porch. She called a doctor who had been at the party.

"There's only one thing to do," he said. "Call everybody and tell them to come to the hospital. I'll go right away and have my stomach pumped out by the time the rest of you arrive."

The embarrassment of the Hendersons knew no bounds. They apologized over and over again. Some of the guests understood and smiled. Others didn't take it too well. The ordeal finally ended at 4:30 a.m. The Hendersons went home last. The dead cat still lay on the back porch, but now Matty noticed a note on the screen door: "Sorry, but I ran over your cat."

910. "Doesn't it embarrass you to go back to the table for seconds so many times?"

"No, I tell them it's for you."

911. Sally didn't get invited to her friend's lawn party. She was pretty put out about it. Just before the party, the error was discovered. Her friend called her, asking her to come to the party.

"It's too late. I've already prayed for rain."

912. My wife and I had to leave the party early. She could hardly keep her mouth open anymore.

7, 237, 892

Past-Due

913. The boss asked his stenographer to write some letters to the firm's past-due accounts. She wrote the letters and brought them in for inspection. The boss looked them over, then suggested that she not use such harsh language. Her second attempt fared no better, so she tried a third time.

"This is better! But do them over just once more, Milly. *Wretched* is spelled with only one *t* and there is only one *l* in *swindler*."

Paternity Suit

914. "Do you remember, dear? We agreed we would share our problems. Do you remember that?"

"Yes."

"Well, we've been named in a paternity suit."

Pedestrian

915. It's safe to walk in outer space, but don't try it on Main Street.

Pennsylvania

916. If business is as good da last six months as it vas da next six months, by golly, son of a gun, I hope so.

917. "Haf some chelly."
"Ephrim, how long vas you in dis country?"
"Ach, some eight years around I dink."
"That long? And you can't even yet say yelly?"

Perfume

918. A lady with a baby in her arms stopped at the perfume counter, where My Sin, Tabu, Ecstasy, Irresistible, and Surrender were displayed.
"Ma'am, would you like a testimonial?"

779, 1278

Personnel Manager

919. The personnel manager was showing the sales manager how to use psychology in employee interviews. The personnel manager called in the first woman.
"What is two and two?"
"Four."
"Thank you." He dismissed her and called in another.
"What is two and two?"
"Twenty-two."
"Thank you." She was dismissed and a third applicant came in.
"What is two and two?"
"It could be four, but it could also be twenty-two."
"Thank you." The third woman left the office and the personnel manager turned to the sales manager.
"Now here we have a clear-cut example of what I have been talking about. The first woman has a conventional mind. The second one has an imaginative mind. The third has both conventional qualities and imagination. Now which of the three will you hire?"
"The one with the tight sweater."

Pessimist

920. A pessimist is an optimist who has just read the latest unemployment figures.

921. She was a misfortune teller.

922. A knocker is a person who gets caught on the losing side.

923. I have a friend who is a pessimist. All she gets out of life, to hear her tell it, is what she eats and what she wears. What she wears, she says, doesn't fit, and what she eats doesn't agree with her gastric system.

924. I haven't made up my mind yet which side I'm on, but when I do, I know I will be very bitter.

898, 1264

Philosophy

925. Don't expect mice to close down a cheese factory.

926. If you want to find big fleas, you have to go where there are big dogs.

927. A scientist placed a bass on one side of an aquarium and a minnow on the other side. The bass immediately gobbled up the minnow. This was repeated a dozen times. Then the scientist placed a glass between the bass and the minnow. The bass went after the minnow, as before, but bumped its nose against the glass. After the bass failed to get to the minnow a dozen times, it gave up. Then the scientist removed the glass. The bass remained at his end of the tank. The minnow remained at the other. The bass had convinced himself that business was lousy.

928. When the backyard hammock went out, ulcers came in.

929. One thing is worse than an old fogey. A young fogey!

930. Smart is to believe half of what you hear. Brilliant is to know which half is true.

931. When all is said and done, more is said than done.

932. Half of the world is wondering how the other half gets away with it.

933. If the do-it-yourself craze continues, it might even filter down to thinking.

934. It wasn't raining when Noah started building the ark.

935. Man does not live by words alone, but sometimes words must be eaten.

936. There's more to grapefruit than meets the eye.

937. Most people would rather lose ten dollars at the race track than a quarter through a hole in their pocket.

938. One day as I sat musing, sad and lonely, without a friend in the world, a wee, small voice came to me saying, "Cheer up, things could be worse." I cheered up and sure enough, things got worse.

939. You don't make hash. It just accumulates.

940. Remain silent and others suspect that you are ignorant. Talk and you remove all doubt of it.

941. If you can keep your head when all others are losing theirs, it is just possible you have not grasped the situation.

942. With friends like him, who needs enemies?

943. You're only young once, but you can be immature all your life.

944. You can always find people who will give three cheers for something they wouldn't give anything else for.

945. Have you ever met an ex-soldier who confessed that he was only a buck private? Have you ever met a politician who admitted he or she made a mistake? Have you ever met a person who went fishing and confessed that he or she didn't get a nibble? Have you ever met an editor that didn't blame the typesetter for mistakes in the paper?

946. Third World countries are short on everything but people.

947. Familiarity breeds contempt, but on the other hand, that's the way everything else is bred too.

948. Watch out when you walk through the cow pasture and the chips are down.

949. Jumping at conclusions is not nearly as good exercise as digging for the facts.

950. A live wire would be dead without connections.

951. Learn from the mistakes of others. You won't live long enough to make all of them by yourself.

952. Fire departments don't fight fire with fire.

953. "If you can't stand the heat, stay out of the kitchen." Harry Truman.

954. Some people are bothered by evil thoughts. I rather enjoy mine.

955. Failure went to his head.

956. The best thing about the past is that it is past.

957. Never look down on a lily because one day a lily will be looking down on you.

958. We live in an age of creeping complexity.

959. When I was young I was told to listen to my elders. Now I'm an elder and I'm told to listen to the young folks. Somehow I missed life along the way.

960. A crowded bus smells different to a midget.

961. Society will reward you if you are an unusual individual, but it will wait until you have been dead for twenty years.

962. Do you ever feel the whole world is wearing a tuxedo and you're wearing brown shoes?

963. The early bird catches the worm, they say, but I don't know of anyone who cares for worms. Do you?

964. The person who wins the car that is being raffled off will either have: (1) one ticket, or (2) one car.

965. No matter how clearly you write or speak, expect somebody to misinterpret what you wrote or said.

966. When the public derides a plumber because his is a humble profession and exalts a philosophy professor because his is a lofty calling, we will get neither good plumbing nor good philosophy.

967. If we do it, it is the voice of experience calling. If somebody else does it, it is either sinful, unethical, immoral, or uncalled for.

968. If you're over forty, unlearn something every day.

969. Don't let yourself be burdened with facts. The facts are probably obsolete anyway. We're moving pretty fast nowadays.

970. Here are some great three-word sentences . . .
I love you.
Keep the change.
You look great.
Sleep till noon.
Please help me.
You've lost weight
Batteries not included.
No, come to think of it, that last one is not so great.

971. Yeats and Shaw were poor spellers.
Franklin, Picasso, Adler, and Jung were poor mathematicians.
Einstein, Poe, Shelly, Roentgen, and Whistler were expelled from school.
Edison was in the bottom half of his class.
Gaugin was a dreamer.
According to his teacher, Watt was dull and inept.
Brothers and sisters, there's still hope for you and me.

972. The best way to look to the future is to do it like the farmer who sights down his row of fence posts before he erects another.

973. "Property is desirable, is a positive good in the world; that some should be rich so that others can be rich too. Let him who is homeless not pull down the house of another, but let him work diligently to build one for himself so that his own may be safe from violence when his house is built." Abraham Lincoln.

974. Poise is the ability to buy new shoes without being self-conscious about the holes in your socks.

975. "If you do not take part in government yourself, you will be ruled by your inferiors." Plato.

976. Hitting the bulls-eye is seldom accomplished by shooting the bull.

741, 1300

Photography

977. She's like a poor photograph—underdeveloped and overexposed.

978. "These pictures don't do me justice."
"You don't need justice. You need mercy."

979. Snow White took a picture of the seven dwarfs and sent the film to be developed. This prompted the song, "Some day my prints will come."

980. My photograph wasn't released. It escaped.

Physiologist

981. A physiologist is a person who watches everybody else when a handsome person walks by.

Plan

982. When Everett Dirksen ran for the Senate, he addressed a school assembly.
"Mr. Dirksen, if you're elected, you will be a Senator. What if you are not elected?"
"I don't plan to lose."

983. A man was building a chimney. The higher he went, the more the chimney leaned. Finally he yelled, "Look out below, I've changed my plans."

168, 490, 909, 1085, 1401

Plastic Surgery

984. I had a scar on my cheek, so I went to a plastic surgeon to remove the scar. He took some skin off my hip and grafted it on my cheek. Now when my mother-in-law kisses me, I smile.

Platform Emergencies

985. When there is trouble with the PA system.

The last time a PA system did not act up throughout an entire convention was at the convention of the Daughters of the Confederacy in Birmingham, Alabama on October 2, 1924.

986. When someone makes a speech instead of asking a question.

Would you please just give us the highlights of your question? Our lease expires next July.

987. When you can't answer a question that is asked.

That can't be very important or I would know the answer.

988. When the lights go out.

Please Con Ed, the check is in the mail.

989. When you have to take a drink of water.

Pardon me. I had some dry martinis last night and some of the dust is still caught in my throat.

990. When you lose your place in your notes.

You're going to be surprised to hear what I'm going to say, and so am I. I've lost my place.

991. When someone flashes a camera in your eyes.

Take another one. I can still see out of my right eye.

992. When there is an obnoxious person in the audience.

Sir (Ma'am), I'll give you a going-away present, if you'll do your part.

993. When somebody walks out.

It's down the hall to the right, second door.

994. When the mike must be raised or lowered.

Let me adjust this gadget for inflation.

995. When you stumble in your speech.

I spend ninety-two dollars to have my eyes fixed and now I have trouble with my mouth.

996.

If they only had erasers for speeches.

997.

There will be a slight pause so that I can open my mouth and put my other foot in.

998. When a story falls flat.   Quietly and without emotion, tear up a 3x5 card and throw the pieces away.

999.   Now that the laughter has subsided . . .

1000.   Scratch the mike and say, "Testing, 1-2-3-4, testing."

1001. When only a few laugh.   Thank you, Mother!

Plumber

1002. While we waited for the plumber to come, we taught the kids how to swim.

1003. "My sink isn't working."
"I'll be right out. Will I need any male and female fittings?"
"I don't want to breed the sink. I just want you to fix it."

966

Police

1004. Lem was taking a pickup full of pigs to market when the cop stopped him.
"Have you got a governor on this truck?"
"No, officer, them's pigs you smell."

1005. He was arrested for selling youth pills. He promised eternal youth to his customers. When the cops booked him at the station house, they checked his record and found that he had been arrested on the same charge in 1772, 1829, and 1904.

64, 76, 81, 89, 161, 217, 335, 360, 594, 838, 851, 901, 1333

Political Parties

1006. You are no longer ostracized if you say you are a Republican in the Deep South. But it wasn't always that way.

Some years ago, the Election Board was counting ballots. They came upon a Republican vote. They found nothing wrong with it, but laid it aside until later. They would make a decision about this ballot after all the other ballots were counted. Suddenly a second Republican ballot showed up.

Judge: "The son-of-a-gun voted twice. Throw them both out."

1007. Everybody's got to eat—even Democrats.
(Or it could be . . .)
Everybody's got to eat—even Republicans.

1008. I am not a member of any organized political party. I'm a Democrat (Republican).

1009. Want ad: Democrat boy wants to meet Republican girl. Object: Third party.

1010. The Bible speaks of Republicans and Democrats. What else does the passage about "publicans and sinners" mean?

1011. If a person leaves one political party and comes to yours, he or she is a convert. If you lose a person to another party, that person is a deserter.

Politician

1012. Show me a politician who has both feet on the ground and I'll show you a person who can't get his or her pants off.

1013. If you are dealt a short suit, remember that politicians do not always play with a full deck.

1014. "I love dogs. They will do nothing for political reasons." Will Rogers.

1015. This is a great year for politicians. There is enough blame to pass around to everybody.

1016. "Son, did you or did you not do this dastardly deed?"
   "Father, I cannot tell a lie. Maybe I did and maybe I didn't."

1017. Chris Columbus was the world's first politician. He didn't know where he was going. He didn't know where he was when he got there. And he did it all on somebody else's money.

1018. Doctor: "Medicine is the oldest profession. God took a rib from Adam and made Eve."
   Lawyer: "But before that God had created law and order, so law is the oldest profession in the world."
   Politician: "Before that there was chaos. Where do you suppose all that chaos came from?"

1019. Beware of those who bear free gifts from the banks of the Potomac.

1020. Since we are so indifferent to political corruption, we are guilty of indecent composure.

1021. I'm for the old-fashioned way, the so-called smoke-filled rooms. That way we would get an open convention.

167, 172, 178, 189, 190, 191, 192, 532, 735, 945, 1144, 1290, 1335, 1347

Post Office

1022. The Post Office: Two hundred years of service unhampered by progress.

1023. Postmaster: "You have a lot more stamps on this letter than you need."

"Oh, I hope you won't send it too far. It's for my sister Mabel in Long Beach."

1024. The idea of fast, reliable, efficient postal service is an idea whose time has come (pause) and gone.

1025. Look what you get for the price of a postage stamp. You put hundreds of people to work for eleven days.

1026. People always complain about slow postal service. When did your phone bill or electric bill ever come late?

193, 689

Poverty

1027. Poverty does not breed crime. The Depression was one of the most crime-free periods in our nation's history.

1028. Poverty is no disgrace, but it's darned inconvenient.

1029. When I was a kid, I didn't have those nice bedroom slippers shaped like a bunny, all fuzzy and stuff like that.

My Mom got my bedroom slippers in Tiedke's Basement for 39 cents. The soles were made of old tire treads. She paid 39 cents plus 10 cents per slipper for balancing. Every birthday I had to take my slippers in to have them realigned.

1030. They are so poor that the kids have to sleep in the box that the color TV came in.

1031. There may have been a wolf at the door, but that didn't scare the stork away.

1032. We were so poor, we had a hoot owl for a watchdog.

211

Pray

1033. God weighs prayer; he doesn't count them.

1034. God, I'm not asking you to move mountains. I can do that with dynamite and a bulldozer. I'm asking you to move me.

1035. "I was driven to my knees when there was no other place to go." Abraham Lincoln.

1036. God bless our happy pad!

36, 221, 274, 373, 604, 911, 1119, 1214, 1268

Precedent

1037. Precedent is the only reason we can give for doing some of the things we do. For instance . . .

How many of you out there in the audience have spouses who keep ketchup and peanut butter in the refrigerator?

How many of you have ever seen spoiled ketchup or spoiled peanut butter?

How many of you *like* cold ketchup and peanut butter?

1041

Pregnant

1038. Susie, at piano lessons, hit a sour note and said, "Pregnant!" The teacher asked why.

"Last night Mother said she was pregnant and Daddy said, "That's a hell of a note."

1182

President

1039. This is a great country. Any kid can grow up to be President. That's the chance he or she has to take.

1040. My neighbor won't believe anything until the President denies it.

1041. Thomas Jefferson had no constitutional right to buy Louisiana from the French for $15 million, but he did it anyway. That set a precedent for constitutional disregard. Unfortunately most of the deals since then haven't been as good as the Louisiana Purchase.

1042. Jimmy Carter had a White House dilemma. What kind of wine do you serve with grits?

1043. "Calvin Coolidge didn't do nothin' but that's what the people wanted him to do." Will Rogers.

1044. "There is no right to strike against the public safety by anybody, anywhere, anytime." Calvin Coolidge.

1045. Uncle Joe Cannon, Speaker of the House of Representatives, said of Teddy Roosevelt: "He has as little use for the Constitution as a tomcat has for a marriage license."

1046. "I shall use my position as President to discuss up and down the country, in all seasons, at all times, the duty of reducing taxes, of increasing the efficiency in governmental structure, of getting the most public service for every dollar paid by taxation. This I pledge you!" Franklin D. Roosevelt.

Come again, F.D.R., I'm not sure I heard you right.

1047. President Wilson parked his private railroad car in Hannibal, Missouri long enough to visit the Mark Twain shrines. Without announcing who he was, he asked one of the folks in Hannibal, "Do you remember Tom Sawyer?"

"Nope. Never heard of any Sawyers."

"How about Huckleberry Finn?"

"They's some Finns down the road apiece, but I don't recklect that there's a Huckleberry among 'em."

"How about Pudd'nhead Wilson then?"

"Yep. Voted for him twice."

107, 242, 290, 1164

Prison

1048. Pen pal, writing to a prisoner: "Dear 688-350. May I call you 688 for short?"

601, 708

Production

1049. When will government learn that you do not get production by pulling rabbits out of a hat? You place two rabbits in a hat and leave them alone.

Profit

1050. I hope we break even this year. I need the money.

1051. It will make more money for me and my company, and I can't think of two more deserving people.

179

Psychiatrist

1052. Anybody who goes to a psychiatrist ought to have his or her head examined.

1053. She always had an inferiority complex. Her psychiatrist found out what was wrong. She really was inferior.

1054. Doc, I'm worried. I don't feel jumpy anymore.

1055. He was so normal that it took the psychiatrist a long time to figure out what was wrong with him.

1056. Psychiatrist to IRS official: "Nonsense, the whole world isn't against you. Maybe all the people in the United States, but certainly not the whole world."

219

Public Relations

1057. John D. DeButts, former chief executive officer of I.T.T., believed in advertising. He made 150 speeches all over the country so that his company's name and his name would become household words. Then Roper took a survey.

Roper found that 2 percent of the people identified DeButts as a corporate official. However, 6 percent thought he was a cabinet secretary, 3 percent thought he was a labor leader, and 1 percent thought he was an astronaut.

DeButts, now desperate, placed his picture in I.T.T. ads. After the ads ran, DeButts is reported to have said, "Now 33 percent of those who identified me as a corporate official knew I was in the communications business. Half of the rest thought I ran a string of ice cream parlors. The other half thought I was a chicken farmer."

Public Speaking

1058. The introduction was admirably correct (pause) except for one omission. Mr. Chairman, you forgot to mention that I have degrees from Vienna, Rome, and Oxford. I have them right here in my pocket. In Vienna it's 68 degrees, in Rome, 78, and in Oxford, 71.

1059. You that are pushing 40, or are dragging it along behind you . . .

1060. Let me assure you that I will not speak of chickens and cattle. This is no cock-and-bull story.

1061. "What did you think about my last talk?"
"I hope so."

1062. As an unprejudiced outsider, what do you think of the human race?

1063. "I talk to you in English and you listen to me in dingbat." Archie Bunker.

1064. There's one part of speech-making recipes that most speakers skip over. The shortening.

1065. I don't mind if you look at your watch when I speak. Just don't shake it to see if it is still running.

1066. Saying this makes me sound like a fool, which I hope I'm not, or a genius, which I know I'm not.

1067. SSCS: Society for Softer Convention Seats.

1068. Lulu got married on Friday and divorced on Monday.
   "That was the most over-introduced man I ever met."

1069. Response to introduction: "I didn't realize until just now that some kind soul has already written my obituary."

1070. As the firefly said as she flew into the electric fan, "I'm delighted (pause) no end."

1071. Paste some dollar bills under chairs in the auditorium, most of them in front. At the end of the speech, ask the people to look for the dollars.
   "See, that proves you have to get off your duff if you want to make a buck."

1072. Last night my wife told me what she always tells me, "Take out the garbage." So, ladies and gentlemen, I have cut this 45-minute speech to 15 minutes.

1073. If people only talked about things they know something about, a great silence would settle on this earth.

1074. I had an unfortunate accident when I was a baby. I fell out of a second-story window and landed on my head. So I've had to get along without the use of my head all these many years.

1075. Beautiful ladies and something less than handsome gentlemen . . .

1076. It is great to see so many beautiful ladies here this evening. You're beautiful, well groomed, well dressed, well coiffed, made-up, and shapely. The men look like charred stumps as usual. But don't get carried away, ladies. I'm a member of Men's Lib. I would like to register a complaint. Men never get mentioned. When you're born, they say, "Wonder how the mother is?" When you get married, they say, "Wasn't she a beautiful bride?" When you die, they say, "Wonder how he left the widow fixed?" Men never get mentioned.

We are born of a woman, learn to speak from a woman, learn our Sunday School and grade school lessons from a woman, then at the time of our Junior Prom, we get our first kiss. I mentioned that at a banquet the other evening and a 12-year-old girl in the front row chirped up, "I got news for him." Then we chase you until you catch us. I was engaged six months before I found out about it. We get married, and get a joint bank account—we put it in, and you take it out. Nowadays that might be vice versa. We make a will, and take out insurance policies, and at age 74, there are 24 percent more women than there are men. At age 74, what difference does that make?

Yes, behind every successful man there is a woman (pause) telling him he's wrong. If you took a man apart to find out what makes him tick, you would find that a woman was the mainspring. Whether we have a nest egg or goose egg at the end of our life depends on the chick we married.

1077. There is a question about whether there is fire in this speech or whether the speech should be in the fire.

1078. My talks are getting more interesting all the time, but as the economists say, "at a declining rate."

1079. He is as pleased as Johnny Weismuller was when he found out that he was Tarzan and not Jane.

1080. When you go home and your friends ask you what kind of speech you heard yesterday, tell them, "It was the greatest speech I ever heard." Then go home and fall on your knees and ask the Lord to forgive you for telling that big fat lie.

1081. Most speakers say, "I'm glad to be here." That is an understatement in my case. I'm thrilled to be here.

1082. Don't applaud. Just throw money.

1083. I'll do as the fan dancer does. Call attention to the subject, but make no great effort to cover it.

1084. It is customary for a speaker to be introduced by a joke. Over in Newport the other night, I was. . . .

1085. We went over the July 4 celebration plans. The mayor said, "I'll talk first and then I'll be followed by Jimmy Newsom, who will recite Lincoln's 'Gettysburg Address.' Then you speak, and then comes the firing squad."

1086. He was only minding everybody else's business.

1087. "Please give a short dissertation on sex."

"OK. How's this! It gives me a great deal of pleasure."

1088. "I was once introduced by a lawyer who had his hands in his pockets. He said I was a humorous speaker who was really funny. When I got up to speak, I replied 'I suspect it is a bit unusual to find a humorous speaker who is really funny, but not nearly as unusual as finding a lawyer with his hands in his own pockets'." Mark Twain.

1089. Now I will answer your questions—to your utter amazement and my complete satisfaction.

1090. I saw the MCs notes. She has me down for twenty minutes. But she wrote below that, "He'll probably go over. The windbag always does."

1091. I have three criticisms of your speech: (1) You read it. (2) You read it poorly. (3) It wasn't worth reading. Alben Barkley

1092. Isn't it ironic? Some people claim they can't sleep in lousy convention hotel beds, and then they fall asleep on stiff chairs during the convention. I give you fair warning. I have an anvil up here that I will pound the moment I see the first of the heavy-eyelid crowd start to nod.

1093. The MC said I need no introduction. I've got news for him. I need all the introduction I can get.

1094. The Roman Emporer asked Androcles how he kept the lions from eating him in the arena.

"That's simple. I just whisper into the lion's ear, 'After dinner, you'll be asked to say a few words.' That shuts their mouths. It works every time."

1095. Don't bother me. I've got to make a speech. This is no time to think.

1096. I'm delighted to be with you here this evening. In fact, at my age, I'm delighted to be almost anywhere this evening.

1097. I knew it was a kinky crowd when somebody yelled during the silent meditation.

1098. "Do you know what a paralleloid is?"

"No."

"Then I can speak freely."

Purchasing Agent

1099. The receptionist took the salesman's card in to the purchasing agent. The purchasing agent tore up the card, and told the receptionist that he didn't want to see the salesman.

Salesman: "Tell your boss these calling cards are expensive. If he doesn't want to see me, I would like my card back."

Secretary to puchasing agent: "He wants his card back."

"I tore it up, but here's a quarter. Give him this."

The receptionist gave the salesman the quarter.

"Tell your boss that the cards are two for a quarter. Here, take this second one in to him."

With that kind of persistence, the salesman finally got to see the purchasing agent (pause) and made a sale.

Q

Quaker

1100. Said the Quaker, "Have a care, my friend, that thou mayest not run thy face against my fist."

1101. A Quaker's cow switched him with her tail, then stepped into the bucket, then kicked the milk bucket over.

"Cow, thou knowest that I love thee and that I would not harm thee. Thou knowest that thou aggravatest me with thy tail. Thou knowest that I would say naught when thou steppeth into the bucket, but what thou did not knowest when thou kicketh the bucket over is that I'm going to sell thee to a Methodist and I hope he kicks the living daylights out of thee."

1102. At a Quaker funeral . . .

"One thing thou canst sayeth about William. At times he was not as bad as he was at other times."

1103. A Quaker heard a burglar in the house. He grabbed his gun and confronted the burglar.

"My religion forbids me to shoot any living thing, so I must needs warn thee that thou standest in the spot where I am about to shoot."

799

Quebec

1104. Faster than an Englishman riding a bicycle through Quebec City waving the Union Jack, singing, "This Land Is My Land."

Question

1105. "Who said, 'I never met a man I didn't like?' "
"It was either Will Rogers or Elizabeth Taylor."

25, 28, 48, 176, 475, 662, 709, 727, 1077, 1089, 1106, 1252, 1255

Questionnaire

1106. Question on government questionnaire: "Have you ever committed suicide?"

Quick

1107. Are you quicker on the deposit than your wife is on the draw?

44, 203, 276, 608, 1244, 1256

Quiet

1108. It's so quiet, I feel like a night watchman at Forest Lawn.

325, 422

Quitter

1109. Two frogs were dropped separately into two cans of milk. As the milk was hauled to town, one frog gave up and died. The other paddled frantically until he had churned a lump of butter. When the lid was opened, there he sat on that lump of butter—all out of breath but with a smile on his face.

Moral: The winner never quits and the quitter never wins.

439, 442, 497, 523, 616

R

Racing

1110. At the race track, they noticed every time the priest made a sign over a horse, the horse won. Next time they bet on the horse over which the priest had made a sign. The horse came in last.

Priest: "You fellows must be Protestants. You don't know the difference between a blessing and last rites."

1111. "I want you to just hold the pace around the first turn. Move up to third on the back stretch. Take second on the far turn, then move into first at the head of the final stretch. Gradually pull away from the field."

The jockey did as he was told; all except that last part about moving into first.

"You didn't follow directions. Why didn't you move into first place like I told you?"

"What? And leave the horse behind?"

1112. A lady at the race track kept asking everyone if they had a safety pin. Nobody had a safety pin. Then someone yelled, "They're off!"

The lady fainted.

74, 79, 937

Radio

1113. Announcer: "Shattered scours predicted for tonight."

1114. "The people I sold Pepsodent to are now using Polident." Bob Hope.

1115. Baseball announcer: "Let me recrap the fifth inning for you, folks."

479, 711, 1307

Railroads

1116. A trainman on top of a train signaled to the engineer with his lantern, then dropped the lantern. A passer-by tossed the lantern back up.

In a moment the engineer came running back all out of breath, "Let's see you do that again."

"Do what again?"

"Jump off the train with your lantern and then jump back up again."

1117. English sign in the Tokyo railroad station: "Baggage shipped in all directions." Our airlines give the same service.

1118. Back in the days when the railroads carried the mail, a man flagged down an express train with a red lantern. The train crew came running to him and he handed the crew a letter. "Here, mail this for me."

"You're crazy. You can't stop an express train to mail a letter."

"But I just did."

433, 478, 503, 780, 1047, 1165, 1336

Raise

1119. "You were going over my head, weren't you?"

"I was not!"

"Yes, you were. You were praying for a raise, weren't you?"

480, 662, 895

Ready

1120. She wore an evening gown and sneakers. She wanted to be ready for anything. Dancing or basketball.

789

Realtor

1121. I went to see my Realtor. I asked him to show me something I could afford. We had a good laugh, and then we got down to serious business.

Recognition

1122. "I like football. It's a contact sport."

"I like basketball. It's played indoors."

"For my money, give me baseball. There're three men on base and you're two runs behind. You come up to bat and the crowd yells, 'You better hit, you bum!' It's that special individual recognition that I like."

Records

1123. He made a 12-inch record. Thank God it had a 10-inch hole.

687, 767, 1005, 1259, 1308

Red Ink

1124. Boss: "What's that red on your fingers?"
Accountant: "Blood."
"Thank God! For a minute I thought it was ink."

Redistribution of Wealth

1125. In our economy we have two means of redistributing great wealth: (1) taxation, and (2) offspring.

Regulation

1126. Government regulations are generally diarrhea of words and constipation of thought.

1127. Army Manual quote: "Tent pegs, aluminum, 9-inch, NSN 8340-00-261-9749 must be painted orange. The bright color provides an easy means of locating the pegs under various light and climatic conditions during field exercises. When orange tent pegs are used, they must be driven into the ground, completely out of sight."

1128. The King James version of the Bible says, "Give us this day our daily bread."

Federal regulators have clarified this sentence: "We respectfully petition, request, and entreat that due and adequate provision be made, this day and date hereinafter subscribed, for the satisfying of these petitioners' nutritional requirements and for the organizing of such methods of allocation and distribution as may be deemed necessary and proper to assure the reception by and for said petition-ers of such quantities of baked cereal products as shall, in the judgment of the aforesaid petitioners, constitute a sufficient supply thereof."

1129. Government has mandated that this message be printed on shaving cream cans: "Wash face, press center top of can to release lather, spread lather evenly over face, shave." Who needs instructions on how to shave? If Thomas Jefferson woke up today, would he ask, "Show me how to shave?"

The next thing you know, government will require this message on soap packages: "Adjust water to desired temperature. Allow sufficient time for water temperature to stabilize. Failure to do so may result in burns or frostbite. Lather the entire body, washing vigorously, rinsing thoroughly. Note: For best results, remove all garments before you bathe."

1130. Government regulations are like a brand new Boy Scout. You go across the street whether you want to or not.

1131. We have a lot of people in Washington, DC who have over-developed regulatory glands.

1132. City ordinance: "All fireplugs must be inspected at least three days before each fire."

1133. Fortunately, people always seem to be able to work around government regulations. If they didn't have this talent, our economy would stop dead in its tracks.

1134. Instead of banning saccharin, why don't we ban the bureaucrats who ban saccharin?

1421

Religion

1135. When three Methodists meet, they talk about the evils of strong drink. When three Roman Catholics meet, they ask where the next Bingo game will be held. When three Lutherans meet, they start a new Synod.

1136. Things are changing in religion . . .

Baptists are starting to hum, "How Dry I Am."

"This Little Piggy Went to Market," has been translated into Hebrew.

The Pope is singing, "Those Wedding Bells are Breaking up That Old Gang of Mine."

1137. "I got religion."

"Are you going to lay off sin?"

"Sure am!"

"Are you going to pay me what you owe me?"

"Now you're talking business. You're not talking religion."

1138. Eve: "You give me a headache."

Adam: "What's a headache?"

1139. He thought that high cholesterol was a religious holiday.

1140. A man asked a priest to bless his Ferrari. The priest didn't know what a Ferrari was. The man then asked a Lutheran minister to bless his Ferrari. The Lutheran pastor didn't know what a Ferrari was either. So the man asked a Unitarian minister to bless his Ferrari.

"Ah, a Ferrari. Four-hundred-thirty-one cubic centimeters. Zero to 60 mph in five seconds. By the way, what's a blessing?"

1141. "This business of religion is just one constant give, give, give."

"Thank you! That is the finest definition of Christianity I have heard in a long time."

1142. "We shouldn't be out here fishing on Sunday morning. We should be in church."

"If I had stayed at home, I wouldn't have been able to go to church anyway. My wife is sick and I would have had to stay home with her."

1103

Reporter

1143. During the Coolidge administration, a cub reporter, the son of one of Coolidge's friends, appeared at the White House. After taking a tour of the building, he was ushered into the Oval Office. In the brief conversation that followed, the cub reporter explained that he was anxious to get a job with one of the Washington news bureaus. Coolidge told the young man to sit in the corner and "watch what kind of job I have." Callers came and went.

When the two were alone again, Coolidge pointed to a plaque on the wall, "See that inscription over there?" The reporter read the inscription and smiled, "That is a very fine tribute, Mr. President. Don't you think so?"

"Don't know. Never read it."

Coolidge knew enough about journalism to know that he had handed the young man a front-page story, if the reporter knew how to write it.

He did, and got a job on a Washington news bureau.

1144. Reporters, keep your pads open and your pencils sharp at all times. Someday, someplace, some politician may say something worth writing down.

1145. The editor told the cub reporter to be brief. The neophyte took the advice literally.

He wrote: "James C. Humphries, 24, looked up an elevator shaft at the Union Hotel this morning to see if the elevator was coming down. It was. Funeral arrangements are not complete."

Research

1146. Research: Looking for the fellow who moved the file.

819

Resign

1147. All people here who object, please raise your right hand and repeat after me, "I resign."

1148. Letter to U.S. Bureau of Indian Affairs.

Dear Sir: I herewith tender my resignation as superintendent of the Hoopla Reservation. I have tried to follow the bureau's orders. I have installed a golf course and "No Parking" signs. The Indians still are not satisfied. The Past Chiefs Council sent a delegation to see me. They want their kids to be given more opportunities. They asked me to hire an archery expert to teach the young braves how to shoot with a bow and arrow. They also wanted their kids to learn how to start a fire by rubbing two sticks together. I couldn't find a Boy Scout executive to show them, so I give up. Yours truly, Oscar Blankenmiddle.

420

Rest

1149. Dear Sir:

Enclosed find a check for two tickets for my wife and me for the Pittsburgh-Philadelphia game. My wife has worked hard and deserves a rest. Give us one ticket behind first base and another behind third base. I need a rest too. Yours truly, Joe Smith.

165, 1259

Restaurant

1150. "Eliminate my eggs."

"Sorry, sir, but the chef broke our eliminator this morning."

1151. It was a very clean restaurant. Even the food tasted like soap.

1152. "Waiter, these veal chops aren't very tender."

"Sir, I used to be a butcher. I can tell you that a month ago those chops were chasing after a cow."

"But not for milk."

1153. "Waitress, I have only a one-hour lunch period."

"I'm busy. I can't stop to talk to you about your labor problems now."

1154. "Yesterday you served me a bigger steak."

"Yesterday you were sitting next to the window."

1155. A diner ordered whole wheat bread and got white bread. The same thing happened a second day. On the third day, the diner ordered white bread, thinking he would get whole wheat bread.

Waitress: "But sir, aren't you the one who always orders whole wheat bread?"

1156. Mabel, the ice cream shop owner, had a cold.

"What kind of ice cream do you have?"

"Vanilla, strawberry, and chocolate," she said hoarsely.

"Do you have laryngitis?"

"No, just vanilla, strawberry, and chocolate."

330, 357

Restitution

1157. "Piggy" Willson of Athens Plow Company, Athens, Tennessee tells of a day when he drove his Model A Ford over the dirt roads of East Tennessee. Just as he topped a hill, a rooster ran out in front of him. He hit it. The rooster was killed. Piggy stopped at the bottom of the hill to get his gas tank filled. The filling station attendant said, "Y'all know ya killed a rooster up yonder?"

"Yes, I know. He ran right out in front of me."

"Well, Mister, that there rooster belongs to tha Widder Smith, one of the most cantankerous females ya ever did fetch up with. Mister, I would be obliged if ya would go up to tha Widder and tell her what ya done. Ah'm willin' ta pay tha charges just ta keep that there old battle-ax from rantin' and ravin' tha rest of tha year 'bout what some tourister did ta her rooster."

"That's all right. I should have stopped anyway. I'll pay."

Piggy went back to the widow's house and rang the bell. When the widow answered the door, he told her about the accident. She said, "Waddya kill him with?"

Piggy pointed to his Model A. The widow replied, "Mister, you don't owe me nothin'. If that there rooster wasn't fast enough to get away from that heap of iron, he wouldn't a bin fast enough to catch a hen anyway."

207

Reward

1158. Ralph pulled the young daughter of a rich industrialist out of the water, saving her life. The girl's father insisted that the hero accept a reward. The hero demurred but the father insisted.

"Well, if you insist, I could use a set of golf clubs."

"How many are there in a set?"

"Twelve."

Six months later, Ralph got this telegram: "Haven't forgotten my promise. Have bought six golf clubs and am dickering on the other six. Of the six golf clubs I have bought for you, four have swimming pools and two have tennis courts."

961

Risk

1159. The professor told us how to avoid the economic risks he avoided by becoming a professor.

203, 354

Robin Hood

1160. Robin Hood told the peasant, "Here's $1,000. I steal from the rich and give to the poor."

"Great, now I too am rich."

"Stick 'em up!"

Russia

1161. An American tourist visiting Russia met a man named Ivan Ivanovich. "I have a beautiful home at the lake with much expensive furniture. I drive a Zis automobile," Ivanovich told him.

"What will your next purchase be?"

"A pair of shoes."

1162. Russia gets four wheat crops a year. One each from Poland, Hungary, Czechoslovakia, and East Germany.

1163. Three comments on Russian justice:

    1. Swift

    2. Certain

    3. We don't want any

1164. An American said he had the freedom to tell the President that he was nuts. The Russian farmer said he had the same freedom. He too could say the United States President was nuts.

1165. If we want to be more like the Russians, we need only . . .

Cut paychecks 80 percent

Move 30 million people back to the farm

Destroy 59 million TV sets

Tear up 14 out of every 15 miles of highway
Tear up two-thirds of all our railroad tracks
Tear down 70 percent of our houses
Rip out 90 percent of our telephones
Close almost all our churches
Find a country that will ship us food

1166. Soviet officer: "What does a good people's soldier do when he hears the command, 'Volunteers forward?' "

"He steps two steps back so as not to get in the way of the people's heroes."

1167. Karl Marx certainly had great dreams for his Russian people when he said, "Shortages should be divided equally among the peasants."

498, 668, 727, 1380

S

Sales Manager

1168. Roy Jenkinson, sales manager, was very insistent on good grammar, good speech habits, and good spelling. Then he got this letter from one of his salesmen:

Dear Boss: I seen this here outfit which they ain't never bawt a dimes worth of nuthin frum us, and I sole them a cupple hundred thowsund dollars worth uv guds. I am now going to Chawgo.

From Chicago, he wrote:

Dear Boss: I cum hear and I sole them a half milyun dollars wurth uv are eqwipmunt.

Jenkinson sent this bulletin to his salespeople in the field:

All Sales Peepul: We ben spendin too much time hear trying to spel insted uv trying to sel. Lets inkreas them sails. I want everybuddy shud reed these letters from Gooch who is on the rode doing a grate job for us and yoo shud go out and do it like he done!

1169. The sales manager of a dog-food company asked his salespeople how they liked the company's new advertising program.

"Great! Best in the business!"

"How do you like our new label and package?"

"Great! Best in the business!"

"How do you like our sales force?"

They were the sales force. They had to admit that they were good.

"OK, then. So we got the best label, the best package, and the best advertising program being sold by the best sales force in the business. Tell me, why are we in seventeeth place in the dog-food business?" There was silence.

Finally a rookie got up and said meekly, "The blankety-blank dogs won't eat the stuff."

678, 919, 1242

141

Salespeople

1170. He must want my order pretty badly. Yesterday, we played golf together. I was in the sand trap next to the green, and he conceded the putt.

1171. "Watcha sellin'?"

"Nothing. And the boss is chewing my tail off."

1172. "Young man, you should feel flattered that I allowed you to come in here. I turned down five salesmen today."

"Yes, I know. I was all five of them."

1173. Salesman: A man who can convince his wife that she would look stout in a fur coat, and that polyester is the generic term for mink.

1174. A super salesman is one who can make his wife feel sorry for the girl who left her compact in his car.

1175. A salesperson has a smile on his or her face, a shine on his or her shoes, and a lousy territory.

1176. "We're satisfied with the paint we're buying."

"I'm sure you are. But I would like ten minutes with you to make you dissatisfied with it."

"You win, brother (sister), come on in."

1177. A book salesman was having little success selling his book, *How to Farm Better and Make More Money*, to farmers. When still another farmer shook his head, the salesman said, "But don't you want to farm better and make more money?"

"Son, I ain't farmin' half as good as I know how now."

1178. Mr. Gotbucks rented a dog at the hunting lodge. The dog's name was Salesman. Salesman was a terrific hunting dog. When Mr. Gotbucks returned the next year, he asked for Salesman again.

"Sorry, he ain't no good any more."

"Why, what happened?"

"We figured he was so good that he deserved a promotion, so we began calling him Sales Manager. Ever since then all he wants to do is sit on his haunches and growl."

1179. Salespeople are big problems to their bosses, to their spouses, to their conservative credit managers, and to hotel clerks. Individually and collectively salespeople are cursed and discussed in sales meetings, conventions, behind closed doors, in bathrooms, and hospitality suites. Salespeople are a tribute to themselves. They draw and spend more expense money with less effort, and get smaller value out of it than any other civilized group on earth with the possible exception of politicians. They come in at the most inopportune times, under the slightest pretext, stay longer under more opposition, ask more personal questions, make more comments, put up with more guff, and take more for granted under greater pressure than any group or body—including the U.S. Marines.

They make more noise and mistakes, correct more factory errors, adjust more differences, hear more grievances, pacify more belligerents, cause more divorces, tell more lies, explain more discrepancies, and lose their calm less seldom than ministers. They live in hotels, motels, buses, and airplanes. They eat all kinds of food, drink every conceivable kind of liquid, both good and bad, and sleep before, during, and after hours.

Salespeople keep the economy moving. We can't do without them. Nothing happens until somebody sells something!

1180. "What's all the excitement about? Why are you throwing things out of the drawers? What have you lost?"

"I finally got an order, and I've mislaid the address of our office."

156, 198, 366, 432, 677, 678, 1099, 1168, 1169, 1242, 1342

Scandinavian

1181. A Texan visited his schoolmate in Minnesota. "How big a spread y'all got up here in Minnesota?"

"Aye got 'bout 462 acres."

"Why, them little bitty old spreads you have here in Minnesota. In Texas I've got a spread so big that it takes all day to drive around it on a tractor."

"Aye had a tractor like dat vunce too."

1182. Oley brought a broken baler part into the farm equipment dealership. The parts man asked, "Who busted this?"

"My hired man."

"Isn't that the same guy that got your daughter pregnant?"

"Ya, he's a clumsy son-of-a-gun, isn't he?"

1183. Coffee: Norwegian gasoline

1184. Lars tried to solder two two-by-fours together and burnt down the lumber yard.

279, 680

School

1185. When I was a kid I was so thin that when I stood sideways the teacher would count me absent.

1186. I remember the day I entered the third grade. I cut myself shaving.

1187. A poinsettia by any other name would be easier to spell.

1188. If you were arrested for being a student, would there be enough evidence to convict you?

1189. I spent two terms in the second grade—Nixon's and Ford's.

1190. Teacher: "Color a duck yellow, and have the duck carry a green umbrella."
    Johnny colored his duck red.
    "Have you ever seen a red duck?"
    "No, but I've never seen a duck carrying an umbrella either."

1191. Teacher: "Name the four seasons."
    "I can think of only two—busy and slack," said the merchant's daughter.

1192. "How many make a million?"
    "Not very many."

1193. With this accelerated education, I took an extra shower and missed my sophomore year.

1194. Student: "I can't understand what you wrote on my term paper."
    Teacher: "I told you to write more legibly."

1195. My high school colors were black and blue, and our school yell was "Ouch!"

1196. "What are we going to do tonight?"
    "Let's flip a coin. Heads we get dates. Tails we go to the movies. If it lands on edge, we study."

226, 377, 540, 826, 884, 894, 899, 904

Scotsman

1197. "How much do you charge to rent a boat to go out on the Sea of Galilee?"
    "$10 per hour."
    "Aye, and I can get a boat for about half that much in Aberdeen, laddie."
    "But these are the waters on which Christ walked."
    "With those prices, nae wonder he walked."

1198. "Do they have cheese in Scotland?"
    "Certainly. Haven't you ever heard of the Loch Ness Muenster?"

1199. At an accident in Scotland, one of the passers-by asked one of the many injured that were lying about, "Has the insurance man been roon yet?"

"No."

"Ah, well then. I'll just lie doon aside ye."

1200. Two Scotsmen were in the bar. They sweated it out to see who would buy a drink. It was a tired and discouraging business. Finally there was a break when Mac said:

"I was stealin' through the wood, peering right and left, when suddenly I saw the bushes move silently and directly in front o' me. I peered again and sure 'nuff, there was a fine fat buck. I up wi ma gun, took careful aim, and in spite of my excitement I shot that deer right in the yours."

"What's yours?"

"Whiskey and soda, thank ye."

Seance

1201. At a seance: "Your father is in Toronto."

"No, my father has been dead for three years."

"No, the husband of your mother has been dead for three years. Your father lives in Toronto."

1255

Secretary

1202. Frank was depressed. He said his wife had hired a new secretary for him.

"Blonde or brunette?"

"Bald."

1203. "I'm sorry, but Mary Ann is sick and won't be at work today."

"All right. Who is speaking, please?"

"This is my mother."

1204. "You fired my secretary without giving her a chance."

"No, I fired your secretary without giving *you* a chance."

1205. Don't worry about getting back to the office soon after you're out of the hospital, Eileen. We are all sharing your work. Ruth is making coffee. Mary is taking up collections for wedding and birthday gifts, and I'm working your crossword puzzles.

1206. Secretaries are getting nosier every day. I have a cure for this trouble. When a secretary says over the phone, "What are you calling about?" I reply, "I'm from the insurance company. Tell your boss that the damage to his wife's car is not very serious."

Or try this one: "Mr. Jones left his American Express card on the bed here in the Sultan's Harem Motel. Should I mail it to his house or the office?"

1099

Sell

1207. Sell and sale are four-letter words—just like love.

1208. He sells more stuff by accident than some of our salespeople sell on purpose.

1209. In the words of that great British admiral, Lord Nelson Apfelbaum: "Don't give up the ship. Sell it!"

1210. One of the best selling jobs in the world is when a girl begins to sell her boyfriend on buying an engagement ring.

1211. When any two people meet, one makes a sale.

443, 496, 517, 671, 678, 1005, 1099, 1101, 1114, 1171, 1177

Senate

1212. The Romans elected a distinguished war horse to the Roman Senate—*Equus Superbus Primus.*

Imagine that! Elected a *whole* horse to the Senate!

1213. An empty cab pulled up before the Senate Office Building and our Senator stepped out.

1214. In the Senate gallery:

"Mother, why does the minister pray for all those people?"

"He doesn't. He takes one look at them and then prays for the country."

1215. "A billion here, a billion there; and it soon runs into real money." Everett Dirksen.

641, 727, 982, 1285

Sermon

1216. Short sermon. "If last night you raised it; if this morning you look like it; then it's pretty likely that that is where you are headed."

1217. A church had IOU's in the plate every Sunday. They varied in size—$5, $10, $25. The amount varied according to the donor's appraisal of the quality of the sermon. The IOU's were always re-deemed.

Then one Sunday, there was a note that said, "You owe me five bucks."

1262

Sex

1218. As the flower said to the bee, "Is that all you ever think about? Pollinate, pollinate, pollinate?"

33, 174, 505, 826, 870, 898, 1087, 1418

Shoe Store

1219. A prospective customer entered the shoe store.
   "Do you have any loafers here?"
   "Yes, three of them. I'll get one to wait on you."

1220. Woman in shoe store: "Ouch! I'll take this pair."

383, 637, 869, 962, 974, 1161, 1175

Small Town

1221. Our courthouse was the back half of Jeff Whittler's gas station.

1222. We had three dogs for a fire department.

1223. Our town was so small that our zip code was 53005½.

1224. We used to resist progress, but not any more. We're getting a new Studebaker dealership next week.

1225. My hometown was twenty minutes below South Bend (pause) by telephone.

1226. It's not the end of the world, but you can see the end of the world from there.

1227. Nothing happened in our town. No, I'll take that back. Three things happened every day: (1) morning, (2) noon, and (3) night.

1228. Our town used to be called Poke Plum. You poked your head out the window and you were plumb out of town.

1229. The next town over from ours was Coffee, Tennessee—population 127 cups.

156, 279

Smart

1230. He's so smart, he can add a five-digit column of figures (pause) from the left.

97, 177, 194, 457, 571, 671, 930

Smart Aleck

1231. I asked Doc what to do to keep my head cold from going down to my chest and he said, "Tie a knot in your neck."

Smoking

1232. There's an organization called Marijuana Anonymous, MA for short. When you crave a drag, call up an MA member. He'll rush right over, hold your hand, talk to you, and the two of you can get stinking drunk together.

1233. What I've been reading about smoking and cancer has caused me to give up (pause) reading.

86, 456, 1021, 1404

Sneeze

1234. Doctor: "If you're sneezing, drink a tall glass of cider at breakfast, lunch, and dinner. Drink another glass before you go to bed."
   "Will that cure my sneezing?"
   "No, but it will make you think twice before you sneeze."

Society

1235. She glided into high society horizontally.

220, 892, 961

Soldier

1236. "I don't mind being camouflaged as a tree stump. I can stand the dogs and birds, but I don't like the squirrels running up my leg hiding acorns in my . . ."
   "Soldier, I'm going to cite you for court martial."

1237. "Do you know whether George Washington was a soldier or a sailor?"
   "He was a soldier, Teacher."
   "How do you know?"

"I've seen pictures of him standing up in the boat while crossing the Delaware. A sailor would know better than to stand up in a boat."

1238. Dear Pa: If you want me to come back to the farm when Uncle Sam says he don't need me no more, here's what you better do. Buy me two of the meanest mules in Arkansas. Name one Corporal and the other Sarge. I'll be glad to spend the rest of my days just telling those two jackasses why I made a mistake when I didn't join the Navy instead of falling for this soldier stuff.

Your loving son, PFC Jasper Higgs.

1239. "Private Jones, what is the first thing you do when you clean your rifle?"

"Check the serial number."

"Why check the serial number?"

"To make darn sure it's my rifle I'm cleaning."

572, 766, 945, 1166, 1354, 1355, 1370

Son

1240. Put on clean underwear, son, just in case you're in an accident.

1241. Father: "What's wrong, son?"

Son: "I can't get along with your wife."

1242. A sales manager can motivate hundreds of salespeople but he can't get his son into a barbershop.

114, 193, 296, 475, 535, 604, 634, 662, 748, 1016, 1238, 1346, 1390

The South

1243. "Where was he from?"

"Miami."

"How do you know?"

"He was always talking about suns and beaches."

1244. A Southerner announced he had been born in Seattle. Then he realized what a terrible thing he had said. He quickly added, "But I was conceived in Birmingham."

1245. Bus driver on tour of Southern battlefield . . .

"Here, a handful of Confederates routed 30,000 Yanks. Here, one fine Georgia battalion annihilated a corps of Yankee troops. Here, two brave Virginians captured a regiment of Northerners."

A woman from New England said, "Didn't the Yanks ever win any battles down here?"

"Not while I'm driving the bus, they ain't goin' to win any, Ma'am."

1246. The difference between a Yankee and a Damnyankee is that the Yankee goes home again.

Speculation

1247. "There are two times in a man's life when he shouldn't speculate. When he can afford it and when he can't." Mark Twain.

Sports

1248. Sports: Where monumental physical exertion is considered play.

1249. The National Safety Council made a study of swimming pools and some startling figures appeared.

1250. I know you didn't learn to play this game until this afternoon, but what time this afternoon?

902, 1284. Also see Baseball, Basketball, Football, etc.

Stage

1251. Victor Borge's name is really Robert Charles Arthur Victor Borge. He dropped the first three names because people were beginning to call him "RCA Victor."

1252. "Why do your plays always have to show obscenity, pornography and degeneration?"

"That's part of life."

"So is diarrhea, but I doubt if diarrhea is the kind of material from which Broadway hits are made."

1253. Director: "Sorry, but I believe we should have a bald man for this part."

The actor took off his wig showing that he was bald.

"Sorry, but you're not very convincing as a bald man."

1254. Jackie was having trouble with his lines for the school play. "Cleopatra, Cleopatra, what have you done?"

Teacher said it was easy, "Just say, 'Cleopatra, Cleopatra,' then take two breaths and say, 'what have you done?'"

On the night of the performance, Jackie followed orders exactly. He spoke his lines: "Cleopatra, Cleopatra, (sniff, sniff) *What* have you done?"

1255. Groucho Marx sat through a seance. Finally the medium asked, "Are there any more questions?"

Groucho replied, "Yes. What is the capital of South Dakota?"

1256. Following the script, Groucho Marx romanced a woman on-stage. Not according to the script, Chico came in with this line, "The garbage man is here."

It was hard to get ahead of Groucho. Quick-witted, he said, "Tell him we don't need any."

1257. Liberace cut himself shaving. His legs are a mess!

1258. New valet: "Mr. Coward, what would you say to a little fish this noon?"

Noel Coward: "Hello, little fishie!"

1259. He was a great singer. He made millions of records. He appeared in the movies and on TV. He starred on the Broadway stage. And on the seventh day, he rested.

71, 189, 203

Stock Exchange

1260. We bought a house for $2,500 when we were first married. Last year we went public and listed it on the New York Stock Exchange.

Subsidy

1261. "The decision to approve a subsidy on sugar will have no effect on the consumer prices, since the subsidy will be paid by the United States Treasury." Jimmy Carter, May 4, 1977.

211

Success

1262. Two boys sat in their father's church one Sunday. During the sermon, Reverend Wright pounded the pulpit and said, "Man shall not fly. Thus saith the Lord." The boys thought their father had misquoted the Lord or had quoted him out of context. At Kitty Hawk, they flew.

1263. Work like a dog, eat like a horse, think like a fox, and play like a rabbit. Then see your vet twice a year. Success is guaranteed!

1264. The optimist's glass is always half full. The pessimist's is half empty. The optimist says, "Please pass the cream." The pessimist says, "Is there any milk in that pitcher down there?" An optimist invented the airplane. A pessimist invented the parachute.

1265. Don't take credit for anything unless you are responsible. An elephant and a flea walked across the bridge together. The flea said, "Man, did we shake that bridge!"

1266. He wasn't doing so well when he had 20-20 hindsight. Success came to him when he developed 20-20 foresight.

1267. Let's say you find a gold coin. You pick it up and notice that there are two more coins under that one. Then you find four coins under the two. You find eight coins under the four. You keep picking up coins until your car is overloaded. Now what do you do?

Do you call your friend Harry and say, "Harry, I have something out here that just may interest you." No! You dash to the phone. You press the buttons at ninety beeps a minute. You're shifting first to one leg, then on the other, and finally Harry comes to the phone. You yell, "Harry, get right out here quick! Like *now*! Never mind your pants. *Come*!"

Just how enthusiastic are you when you sell your business proposition?

1268. When you see a picture of a Pilgrim at prayer, note the musket that he has beside him. He wants to be sure of success.

1269. Coming in second is like kissing your sister. Nothing happens.

1270. Success is revenge against those who thought you couldn't do it.

1271. Friends, countrymen, and fellow refugees from bracket creep: Here is a line from Emerson that you may want to paste in your hat. "Do the thing you fear, and the death of fear is certain."

1272. Run like hell, but run in the right direction!

1273. If you trade dollar bills with someone, you both still have what you had. If you trade ideas, each of you will have two ideas.

1274. You are the vice president in charge of a better tomorrow.

1275. If you want to succeed, get off your saturated fatty acids.

1276. Seven ways to elude success:

    1. Don't look—you might see.
    2. Don't listen—you might hear.
    3. Don't think—you might learn.
    4. Don't make decisions—they might be wrong.
    5. Don't walk—you might stumble.
    6. Don't run—you might fall.
    7. Don't live—you just might die!

100, 406, 517, 599, 809, 1177

Sunbathing

1277. A young woman asked if she could sun herself on the roof of the hotel. The hotel manager said it would be all right, but later he changed his mind.

"But you said I could come up here and sunbathe."

"Yes, I know. But I didn't know that you were going to sunbathe everything. And I didn't know that you would sunbathe on the skylight over the dining room."

Superior

1278. The human animal is not superior to other animals. The human animal doesn't even like its own smell. Last year $20 billion was spent on deodorants and perfume.

Surgeon

1279. "Doc, I'm rushing my wife to the hospital. She has acute appendicitis."

"But I took your wife's appendix out two years ago. People don't have two of them."

"But some people have two wives. This is my second wife and believe me, she has appendicitis."

1280. "Doctor, will the scar show?"

"That, my dear young lady, is entirely up to you."

1281. "Give me a double Scotch please, bartender."

"Comin' right up, Doc."

"Whoops, I'm sorry. I spilled it."

"That's okay. I'll pour you another one."

"My, this sure tastes good."

"What are you doing now, Doc?"

"Same old thing—brain surgery."

358. Also see Doctor, Hospital

Survey

1282. Stanford University took a survey. It found 48 percent women, 42 percent men and 10 percent undecided.

Suspicion

1283. Adults who never eat ice cream are instantly suspect. They probably hate sand, sleep in pajamas, never eat spareribs or pizza, and kiss with their mouths closed to keep from getting germs. What a life that must be!

64, 508, 940

Sweat

1284. This is the only country in the world where sweating is considered a sport or hobby.

T

Talkative

1285. She makes a filibustering Senator look tongue-tied!

1286. He talks so much, even his tongue is tanned.

1287. Talk is cheap. Supply always exceeds demand.

70, 268, 607, 624, 658, 705, 723, 873, 892, 1061, 1063, 1073, 1078, 1084, 1243, 1388

Taxes

1288. When your ship comes in, count on government to dock it.

1289. Congress is talking about tax relief, but they're not talking about fast, fast relief.

1290. The Lord bless the I.R.S. which turneth the labors of mankind to naught. We thank thee for 1040 and its multiplicity of supplements. Thou magnifiest the riches of politicians, accountants, consultants, and barristers alike. Grant that my sacrifice shall be sufficient for the auditors.

1291. We have much to be thankful for in this country. Each April 15 we find out how much it costs, too.

1292. Taxes are getting frightful. If they tax whiskey and cigarettes and cars anymore, they're going to lose the entire smoking and drunk-driver vote.

1293. Just because Herbert Hoover gave all his salary back to the government is no sign that the rest of us want to do it too.

1294. New song: "Deep in the Heart of Taxes."

1295. Death and taxes may be inevitable, but death doesn't get worse with each new session of Congress.

1296. The Bible says that the meek shall inherit the earth. But the Bible was written before estate taxes were placed on the books.

1297. Kids are pretty sharp nowadays. One said, "I pledge my allowance to the flag . . ."
She didn't know how true that statement was.

1298. If taxes were voluntary contributions, like church collections, how many of you in this audience would pay 100 percent of the taxes you pay now?
(Note: I've asked this in many a speech and have yet to see a hand go up. In fact, few hands go up when I say "50 percent of the taxes you pay now.")

1299. The American taxpayer: An endangered species.

510, 689, 691, 1046, 1125, 1343

Taxi

1300. A cabbie in Pittsburgh had a great philosophy. She said, "Frank Sinatra came to town and 10,000 people paid $10 each to see and hear him. He paid $14 to see and hear me. He rode in my cab."

1301. Winston Churchill hailed a cab to go to the BBC, where he was scheduled to broadcast a speech to the world.
"Sorry, sir. Ye'll 'ave to get yourself another cabbie. I can't go that far."
Churchill asked the cabbie why his operations were so limited.
"They hain't hordinarily, sir. But ye see, Guvner, Mr. Churchill is broadcasting in an hour and I wants to get 'ome to 'ear 'im on the wireless."
Churchill was so pleased that he pulled out a one-pound note and gave it to the cabbie. The cabbie took one look at the money and said, "Hop in, Guvner. T'hell with Mr. Churchill."

1302. A man of the cloth came to town. He told the cabbie to take him first to the haberdasher.
"Haberdasher. Haberdasher? Mister, is that liquor or is it women?"

1303. After the crash . . .
Woman: "But I gave the right signal."
Cabbie: "Yes, that's what confused me."

Teens

1304. "I know that this is the first time that you've been teen-agers, but remember that this is the first time that your mother and I have been parents of teen-agers."

1305. Good old days: When a teen-ager went to the garage and came out with the lawn mower.

1306. "How do you get your son to mow the lawn?"
   "We tell him that we lost the car keys in the grass."

1307. Teen-agers listen to radio, TV, and stereo, but not to reason.

1308. I took my kids' 12-inch long-playing rock records and drilled a 13-inch hole in them.

466, 728

Telephone

1309. I even get busy signals from sea shells.

1310. There is life on Mars. When NASA called, they got a busy signal.

1311. When your daughter gets married, you do not lose a daughter. You gain a telephone.

466, 468, 556, 565, 690, 720, 1026, 1165, 1206

Television

1312. TV is wonderful. Years ago we could go to a movie for 35 cents. Now we can see that same movie on a $500 TV set—free!

1313. Said a CBS executive: "The C stands for class!"
   Replied an NBC executive: "And the BS?"

1314. Before TV, we didn't know what a headache looked like.

1315. If you think you've had a bad day, wait till you hear what happened on my favorite soap opera today.

1316. "I have a wife and a TV set and both of them work."
   "You lucky stiff!"

327, 479, 544, 596, 736, 874, 1030, 1165, 1259, 1307

Temptation

1317. The only way to get rid of temptation is to yield to it. At least that's the fun way to do it.

879, 904

Texas

1318. Dizzy Dean about Texas: "It ain't braggin' if you can do it."

1319. Texas! It has more rivers with less water and more cows that give less milk. You can stand in one place in Texas and see more of nothing than anywhere else in the country.

1320. A Texan with long legs was sleeping in the aisle seat. The little fellow from Wisconsin who sat next to the Texan got air sick. He couldn't get over those long legs, so, helplessly, he vomited all over the Texan. When the Texan woke up, the little shrimp said, "I hope you're feeling better now."

1321. George Washington actually lived in Texas. He chopped down a mesquite tree. When his father asked who had chopped down the tree, George said, "I cannot tell a lie. I chopped down the mesquite tree with my little hatchet."

"If you cain't tell no lie, son, you ain't got no business in Texas."

1322. Two Texans went into a Cadillac dealership. One picked out a car he wanted to buy.

"Here, let me pay for it. You picked up the breakfast check."

1323. Honey, will you get the car out of the garage and take the kids out so that they can play in our back yard?

1324. A Texan came into Oklahoma roaring drunk. He bedded himself down. The next morning he woke up to find a partner in bed with him.

"Who are you?"

"Ah doan know who Ah is dis mornin', but las night Ah was your yellow rose of Texas."

Another head popped up out of the other bed. She said, "Yassuh, an Ah was da bridesmaid."

1325. "Roll the windows down."

"What and admit here in Dallas that we don't have air conditioning?"

1326. Alaska may be the biggest state, but Texas is the tallest. They have dust storms that go up 30,000 feet.

1327. A short Easterner was with a bunch of six-foot Texans in Houston.

"How do you feel?"

"Like a dime among nickels."

1328. "You can take a bus in Texas and twenty-four hours later, you will still be in Texas."

"Yes, we have slow buses in Illinois too."

565, 900, 1181, 1294

Tip

1329. "What's the average tip here?"
  "Two dollars."
  "Here's your two dollars."
  "Thank you. You are the first person who ever came up to the average."

1330. "Here's $5. Break if for me so I can give you a tip. I need change."
  "Mister, in this fancy place, $5 is change."

641

Topless

1331. These topless outfits. If you've seen one, you've seen them both.

Tourist

1332. Tourist: A person who travels to find things that are different, but comes home to complain that there were no Holiday Inns, McDonalds, or Pizza Huts.

1157, 1161

Traffic Light

1333. A woman with ten kids in the station wagon, ran a stop light. An officer pulled her to the curb.
  "Don't you know when to stop?"
  "These aren't all mine, Officer. Six of them belong to the neighbors."

84

Transplant

1334. Did you read in the paper about the world's first successful hernia transplant at our state university's medical school?

1335. Medical science has been able to transplant hearts, kidneys, and bone joints. Wouldn't it be great if they could graft some guts into our politicians?

Trial

1336. The railroad had been sued in connection with a motorist's death.

Watchman: "The night was dark. I waved my lantern at the railroad crossing like I was supposed to do. This here motorist kept coming. Then the train hit him."

The railroad won the case. The railroad's attorney told the crossing watchman, "You did wonderfully well on the witness stand today. At first I thought you might waver in your testimony."

"No, sir. But I sure was scared that that other lawyer was going to ask me if my lantern was lit."

Truck

1337. My Ford pickup has a sign on the back: "Follow me for genuine Ford parts." The Chevy dealer painted the sign.

1338. A trucker went under a thirteen-foot-three-inch bridge with a thirteen-foot-ten-inch load.

Cop: "What do you think you're doing?"

"I'm delivering a bridge, but I forgot where it is supposed to go."

17, 75, 671

U

Uncle Sam

1339. Uncle Sam: The original Superman!

1238

Unemployment

1340. I wish my brother would learn a trade so that we could tell for sure what kind of work he is out of.

202, 211, 596

Union

1341. The union wanted a right-not-to-work clause along with a still-get-paid clause in the new contract.

351, 1057, 1153

Used Cars

1342. Used-car salesman: "Buy this car. The monthly payments will be less than the repair bills."

Utopia

1343. Utopia: Current wages, 1926 dividends, 1932 prices, and 1910 taxes. Don't dream about it too long. It's as impossible as making birth control retroactive.

V

Vegetarian

1344. Vegetarians have a high mortality rate after age 90. A surprising number of them get run over by meat trucks.

Veterinarian

1345. "My bull wouldn't breed, so I went to Doc Nelson and got some pills for the old critter. He's sure going to town now since I give him the pills that doc sold me."

"What kind of pills are they?"

"I don't know. Doc didn't say, but they taste like peppermint."

408, 1263

Vice President

1346. A woman had two sons. One went to sea. The other became vice president of the United States. Neither has been heard from since.

24, 469, 1274

Vote

1347. A politician came home to find a man hiding in the shower. The politician angrily ripped the curtain aside. The man in the shower said, "Stop that! How dare you interfere with a man while he is voting?"

1348. I voted for Smith. I adore the very quicksand he walks on.

1349. I want to thank all 652 of you for the 3,878 votes you cast for me.

1350. They had a fire in Chicago's City Hall. Too bad! Burned up next year's election returns.

1351. "Preacher, I believe you would vote for the Devil himself if he was on the Democrat ticket."

"Not in the primary, I wouldn't."

213, 603, 701, 812, 1006, 1047, 1292

W

Waltz

1352. Could you waltz a little faster, dear? This waltz is a rhumba.

War

1353. The Englishmen fought to the last Frenchman.

1354. The reason there are so many trees along the roads of France is that German soldiers like to walk where it's shady.

1355. In a war, you can always recognize the front. The soldiers are dirty and the weapons are clean.

1356. Aunt Miranda stood in the middle of the road with a poker in her hand as a Union cavalry unit came toward her.
    "You don't expect to stop us with that poker, do you?"
    "No, but by the time I'm done, you'll know which side I'm on."

1357. "Where is the best place to be when an atomic bomb drops?"
    "Somewhere where people will say, 'What in the heck was that noise?' "

1358. Believe it or not, some people consider war an act of God.

83

Washington DC

1359. In some quarters, Washington, DC is known as Disneyland-on-the-Potomac.

1360. Washington, DC: Sixty-seven square miles of land surrounded by reality.

1361. I spent three weeks in Washington one day.

1362. If I ever go bananas, I hope it will be in Washington. I won't be noticed there.

42, 632, 708, 1131

Wedding

1363. The delightful old custom of getting married in Mother's wedding dress is no longer valid. She's using it when Grandma isn't.

1364. The woman nudist stayed in the shade until after the wedding. She wanted to be married in white.

1365. People seldom think alike until it comes time to buy a wedding gift.

251, 340, 618, 637, 638

Welfare State

1366. Two fleas, while on their honeymoon, found a big inactive dog on which to make their home. The dog provided food, shelter, and heat. It seldom scratched. In this perfect economic climate, the fleas multipled rapidly.

    The dog grew old and weary before his time. One day he trudged into the woods and passed on to the great kennel in the sky.

    One flea yelled, "The economic system has let us down." Some panic-stricken fleas died right on the spot. Others died while hitch-hiking to another dog.

    With a reasonable amount of initiative, a will to do a day's work, a bit of discipline, and self-reliance, the fleas would be living today.

    And so would the dog!

1367. Back in FDR's day, a WPA crew went out to a job site and found they had forgotten their shovels. One man went back to town for the shovels and the rest leaned against each other.

596

The West

1368. "I hear somebody shot up the Palace Bar last night."

    "You heard right, Pardner."

    "What were the reasons?"

    "Reasons? Is this here burg gettin' so blamed civilized that a fellow's got to have a reason for every little thing he does?"

1369. "Where's the men's room?"

    "Just go through that there door, Pardner. There is four thousand acres of rest room out there."

419

West Point

1370. "I beg your pardon, sir. Could you tell me what this monument commemorates? It has only names of Union soldiers on it."

Cadet from Alabama: "That, suh, is a tribute to the mahksmanship of the Confederacy."

56

Widow

1371. Marooned in a snowstorm, two men stayed with a widow. Nine months later, one got a letter.

"That night we were socked in by the snowstorm, did you go downstairs and sleep with that widow?"

"Yes, I'll have to admit that I did."

"And did you give her my name instead of your own?"

"Yes, I'm sorry."

"Nothing to be sorry about. She died and left me her farm."

632, 647, 715, 826, 1076, 1157

Wig

1372. "It looks like you're wearing a wig."

"It is a wig."

"Funny, you'd never know it."

1373. I bought a wig, but somebody shot it during the pheasant hunting season.

1374. Wig: Ear-to-ear carpeting.

1375. The new wigs don't need upkeep, but then neither do the barbed wire and straw bales they resemble.

1376. "Your hair is beautiful."

"Thank you. It's my sister's."

1253

Will

1377. Being of sound mind, I spent the money on myself.

386, 715, 1076, 1371

Will Power

1378. I have an overdeveloped will. I'm looking for a girl with an underdeveloped won't.

Wisconsin

1379. Down in Florida they have a Wisconsinites-in-Florida Club. Every year, the club holds a picnic. They draw for three door prizes. Third prize is a two weeks all-expense trip back to Wisconsin. Second prize is a one week all-expense paid trip back to Wisconsin. First prize is you don't have to go back to Wisconsin.

Wish

1380. Russia's Chernenko, China's Xeng, and Poland's Walesea arrived in heaven. They were given one wish. Andropov wished that there would be a massive earthquake in China. Xeng wished that there would be massive floods in Russia. Walesea said that his two wishes were already taken, so he wished for a cup of coffee.

603, 639

Women

1381. "When I get down in the dumps, I buy some new clothes."
  "I've always wondered where you got your clothes."

1382. I'm sure our dear departed Hazel went to heaven, but I'm just as sure that she won't like God.

1383. When she's out, she dresses like Nancy Reagan. When she's home, she dresses like Mrs. Chernenko.

1384. "He's tall, with dark, curly hair, and he has the sweetest smile. His name is Harold, and just before he kisses me, he always says, 'I'm about to kiss the most beautiful girl in the world.' "
  "Oh, *that* Harold."

1385. She had two children by her first husband, two children by her second husband, and the fifth child came all by itself.

1386. If you want to know a woman's age, ask her sister-in-law.

1387. A woman lies awake hearing strange noises after she reads that a psycho escaped 1,500 miles away, but she doesn't panic when the baby has colic. When she doesn't feel good, she goes to a doctor, which is more than you can say about a man.

1388. Her father was an auctioneer and her mother was a woman. Any wonder she talks so much?

1389. Women can't read a slide rule, can't follow a road map, can't remember what beats what in poker. Women can't tell you what model car they drive.

But women can remember the organdy dress they wore at the Junior Prom. Women can mentally multiply sixteen people by 2½ sandwiches each while ironing a shirt, helping one of her kids write a letter to Santa Claus, and listening to the other kid practice chords on the piano.

1390. She wore a son suit. Her son is 4½.

1391. Red China may be all right, if you have a yellow tablecloth.

1392. Ma'am, do you want to take the package with you, or should I send it directly to the exchange Department?

1393. "Where did you get that black eye?"
"From my husband."
"But I thought your husband was out-of-town."
"So did I."

1394. The best way to get real enjoyment out of gardening is to put on a wide straw hat, dress in a thin, loose-fitting blouse and skirt, hold a little trowel in one hand and a cool drink in the other and tell your husband where to dig.

1395. When a woman wears shoes with the toes missing, she is considered stylish. When her husband tries it, they call him a bum.

1396. She had a figure like an hourglass, only the sand was at the wrong end.

1397. It isn't so much the men in your life as the life in your men.

1398. She made a millionaire out of that man. Before she married him, he was a multi-millionaire.

1399. Just think, in twenty years the gals in this audience will all be five years older.

1400. Engineers are baffled about the fact that the most streamlined girls often offer the most resistance.

1401. Her meals are not planned; they're premeditated.

1402. "I got up in the movie five times to change seats."
"Did somebody bother you?"
"Yes, finally, in the fifth seat."

1403. She was so bow-legged that when she sat around the house, she sat around the house.

1404. Smoking cigarettes makes a woman's voice shrill and harsh. If you don't believe that, just drop a lighted cigarette on some woman's new carpet.

1405. They thought and thought about an appropriate epitaph for Effie's tombstone. Finally someone came up with this bright idea . . .

"At last she sleeps alone."

1406. You can always tell whether a woman is shopping or if she intends to buy. If she asks for something cheaper, she's ready to buy. If she asks to see something more expensive, she's shopping.

1407. Sign in machine shop: "Girls, if your sweater is too loose, watch out for the machines. If it is too tight, watch out for the machinists."

1408. When a diplomat says "yes," he means "maybe." When he says "maybe," he means "no." And if he says "no," he's no diplomat.

When a lady says "no," she means "maybe." When she says "maybe," she means "yes," and if she says "yes," she's no lady.

1409. Men would be better off if they just enjoyed their women instead of trying to understand them.

1410. The skin men love to touch is the skin that women love to retouch.

1411. Last night I dreamed John was out with a blonde, and he was smiling and purring in his sleep. If he does that in my dreams, imagine what he does in his.

1412. If Wanda Schultz had married Howard Hughes, then divorced, then married Henry Kissinger, her name would be Wanda Hughes Kissinger now.

1413. Bridge club: Data-processing center.

1414. Can you open your closet without injuring yourself?

1415. The greatest water power on earth is a woman's tears.

1416. She had a wonderful mind (pause) until she made it up.

45, 104, 105, 146, 185, 261, 282, 297, 314, 327, 331, 411, 412, 419, 429, 491, 500, 551, 553, 560, 593, 605, 612, 623, 680, 709, 733, 791, 863, 898, 1076, 1112, 1220, 1282, 1302, 1333, 1346, 1382

Women's Lib

1417. You'll know that women's lib has gone too far when you hear someone say, "Women the lifeboats," or "Let's sing Number 136 in the blue *her* book."

1418. If you look into the diapers of a baby boy and a baby girl, you will note that there is a difference, a difference which becomes more pronounced as the years go by. Some today view this as a mistake on the part of the Creator. They feel that sexes should be equal. My sympathy to the woman who wants to be the same as a man. If she isn't happy as a woman, believe me, she would not be happy as a man either.

X

X-ray

1419. Before Ernie Kovacs went into X-ray, he cut the letters, "out to lunch" out of tinfoil, and pasted them on his stomach.

1420. He's an X-ray technician, and I don't know what he sees in that girl.

Z

Zoo

1421. "This is a beautiful new lion cage here in the Los Angeles Zoo. How wide is the moat?"
"Eighteen feet."
"But a lion can jump twenty feet."
"He wouldn't dare. It's against government regulations."

Conclusion

Humor abounds. The daily newspaper always provided a ready source of fun for Will Rogers. The current scene also can be mined for humorous material.

When we typed the manuscript for this book, we were amused at some of the chapter headings that were side-by-side. For instance:

Baby and Baby Sitter certainly fit together but how about Bad Luck and Bald?

Some of us wish that Budget and Bureaucracy weren't quite so chummy. Inevitably Committee, Complaint and Compliment are associated.

If the pollsters are correct, Confidence and Congress are not next of kin. And whoever heard of Congress coming up with Conservation?

Courtesy and Courtship are go-together musts.

Dating and Daughter go together like daughter and telephone.

You pick it up from there. Every one of those associations could be woven into a original humorous recess in your speech or script.

PHRASE CROSS REFERENCE

A

Accident. It was a fortunate - 276
Accident. It was an unfortunate - 1074
Achievement. How-to - 11
Acquainted. Let's get better - 778
Adjust to change! - 201, 208
Advertising. Do not use deceptive - 189, 1261
Advertising pays! - 250, 647, 1009, 1337
Adds up. It all - 724
Advantages. Look at your/our - 725
Adversity. Growing up with - 1195
Advice! Good - 1247
Age. We live in a new - 958
Alibi season. It's - 458, 1142, 1150
All right. We're going - 767
Alternatives. There are - 1125, 1196
Alternatives. There are no - 1035
Alternative? What if you had an - 1298
Amazing work! - 625, 842
Answer for everything. He/she has an - 323, 324,
527, 640, 1089, 1279
Answer. Ask a silly question and you get a silly -
1231, 1258, 1338
Answer. That's the right - 488, 530, 549, 618, 627,
668, 718, 750, 1124, 1176, 1303, 1405
Answer. That's the wrong - 127, 306, 527, 621, 704,
717, 726, 729, 1194
Anti-social. You're - 45

Apple polisher! - 1235
Appropriate. Say something - 585, 1405
Argue. He/she's right so don't - 759
Arithmetic. Faulty - 209
Around it? Isn't there a way - 733
Ask. You'll never know until you - 81, 434
Asked for it! You - 1047
Assumption. That was a mistaken - 3
Attention. Get their - 65
Austerity program. We had an - 1222
Average. Come up to - 1329
Awful? Ain't it - 195, 1294, 1296
Axioms. Business - 836, 837

B

Babes. Out of the mouth of - 216, 218
Backfired. Our strategy - 499
Bad! Too - 792, 826, 1396
Bags were loaded. The - 136
Bargain fairly with the customer! - 588
Barnum was right! - 632
Batteries not included. - 970
Battle. It's a losing - 1147, 1148
Beat you/me to it! You - 762
Beats those . . . This sure - 40
Best of everything. Make the - 891
Best. You deserve only the - 49
Bed-bug letter. Send the - 642
Believe it or not! - 575, 581, 827, 901, 1040, 1280,
1315, 1349, 1350, 1351, 1358
Better tomorrow. Build for a - 1274
Better way. There is always a - 395, 546, 641, 682,
1377, 1378
Beware of free gifts! - 1019
Big bad? Is - 152
Big head. Don't get the - 96
Big! What we have is really - 34, 1322, 1323, 1326,
1369
Blood, sweat and tears. I offer you only - 259

C

Compliment club! Join the - 368, 753, 816, 970, 1059, 1075, 1376

Compromise. We'll accept - 353

Conclusions. Don't jump to - 907

Confidence. We need more - 314, 315, 417

Confirmed. The message is - 551

Confused, join the club. If you are - 418, 420, 849, 860

Conscience bothered him/her. His/her - 589

Conserve. We must - 80, 82

Constitutional disregard. - 1041, 1045

Constructive or destructive? - 148

Consultant. Now he/she's a - 325, 326

Convict you? Could they - 1188

Convictions. Be a master of your - 1356

Convincing. That's not - 1253

Correct. That's almost - 1058

Cost? What does it - 1291

Country! We have a great - 1039

Courage! Have - 437

Cover! Don't blow your - 267

Credit. Extending - 405

Credit. We did the work and they get the - 820, 1265

Crisis. Don't add more - 592

Culture! Welcome to - 363

Custom. We will follow - 808

Customer is king/queen! The - 327, 338, 435

Customer what he/she wants. Give the - 493, 623, 1043, 1302

Customers have had it up to here. Our - 256, 511

Customers like you. I wish I had more - 366

Customers are not satisfied. Our - 430, 440

Customers are satisfied. Our - 398, 401, 1220

D

Dare you? How - 1347

Data processing center. - 1413

Dead-beats. Watch out for those - 5, 7, 8

Deal. We got a better - 643
Debt! Avoid - 357, 358
Deception does not pay off. - 1371
Declining rate. At a - 1078
Deeds. Known by their - 126
Define terms! - 690, 1141, 1246, 1374, 1413
Delighted! I am - 1069, 1070, 1079, 1081, 1087, 1096
Dense. He/she is a little - 459, 461
Devil. He/she's a little - 687
Did it! He/she - 1116, 1118
Difference. Know the - 1110
Difference of opinion. We have a - 271, 626
Difference. Thank God for the very little - 822, 1246, 1395
Difficult! It's not all that - 449, 538
Difficult! It's so - 480, 587, 1299
Dilemma. We all face - 87, 176
Diplomatic! Be more - 372
Direction! Go in the right - 95, 390, 613
Directions? Why not follow - 1111
Disaster! - 1184
Discipline. Self- - 470, 471
Discovery! A great - 732, 828
Disguise the obvious. - 814
Disregard the previous message. - 903
Dividends. Create - 215
Do it my way! - 271, 329, 1145
Do it over! - 624
Done. It's already been - 266
Doublecrossed. I was - 301
Drawback. There's one - 80
Drawing board! Back to the - 490
Dream on! - 72, 121, 164, 170, 465, 1167
Drink anything. They will - 49
Drive carefully. - 17, 52
Druthers. If I had my - 610
Duff! Get off your big fat - 1071

E

Early bird catches the worm. The - 10, 213, 963
Ease. Put people's minds at - 21
Easy nowadays. It is - 336
Easy way. Do it the - 567
Easy. That's not - 4
Easy? Who said it would be - 197, 316, 317
Economic recovery. On the way to - 758
Economic recovery. Not on the way to - 760, 834
Economize. We must - 558, 559, 835
Ego was knocked down a peg. His/her - 1047
Ego! Too much - 955, 967, 1259
Elders. Listen to your - 959
Embarrassing. It's - 1347
Emotions. We have mixed - 371
Employee discipline. We need more - 284
Employee relations. - 497
Enjoy! Enjoy! - 954
Enterprising individual. He/she is an - 1199, 1200
Enthusiasm! Build your - 1267
Escape. That was a narrow - 1336
Even. Let's get - 22, 24, 83, 800, 1270, 1308
Even. That makes us - 1217
Everything went fine, and then . . . - 781
Exaggeration. That is slight - 186, 187
Executives have it soft! - 467
Expect it! - 965
Expense books. Let's discuss your - 473
Expensive. You're awfully - 397
Experience is the best teacher. - 474, 1304
Experts don't need it all spelled out. - 106
Explanation. There's always an - 299, 426, 590, 591
Eyes open. Keep your - 751

F

Failure. Achieving - 163, 304, 468, 478, 1276, 1325
Fair. In all things, be - 415, 806

Faith. A test of - 257
Facts are facts! - 263, 631, 744, 761, 791, 868, 946,
947, 1007, 1008, 1237
Facts. Get the - 456
Fame has spread. Your - 809
Familiarity breeds something or other. - 1048
Far. That's going too - 1417
Fast! That's - 1104
Fault? Who is at - 309, 689, 1020
Favors. Thanks for the - 743
Fear. Do the things you - 1271
Fear! Have no - 29, 35
Fellow human being. Serve your - 147
Fight it out! You - 777, 1353
Fight fire with fire! - 508, 952, 1206
Figures! That - 801, 841, 925, 926, 931, 932
File? Who moved the - 1146
Fill his/her shoes. It's easy to - 96
Filling. Life can be - 379
Firing squad. Then comes the - 1085
First choice. You/it were/was not our - 672
First class! Go - 518, 804
First prize is . . . - 1379
Fiscal responsibility. Let's have a little more - 5, 7
Flunked out. - 812
Fooled! Don't let yourself be - 895
Forget it! - 278
Fortunate. We/you are most - 503, 752, 775, 853,
1208
Fortune? Want to make a - 547
Four-letter words. You should use these - 1207
Fraud! - 1006
Free gifts. Beware of - 1019
"Free ink." Go for the - 630
Free market at work. - 1049
Friends really are. That's when you find out who
your - 557
Front-page story! - 1143
Full deck. Deal from a - 1013

Fun! Have - 795, 1284
Fun. That's no/not - 237
Futility. Record in - 133

G

Gamble. It's a - 856
Genius I am not. A - 1066
Give a lot to . . . I'd - 121
Give up! Don't - 349, 1209
GO! - 58, 66, 194, 604
Go together. Things must - 1391
Goal achieved. Another - 160, 379
Goal. Further and further from our - 571
Goals! Set your - 377, 390, 579
Goldbrick. He/she's a big - 633
Good news and bad news. - 210, 227, 611
Good news tonight! - 664, 789
Good old days are gone. - 33, 710, 1305
Good old days were not all that good. The - 1029
Good old place. It's still a - 596
Good. Still pretty - 174
Goofed! We/I - 134, 138, 205, 220, 230, 244, 276,
365, 381, 451, 453, 498, 528, 542, 550, 607, 1113,
1115
Got me there! You've - 67
Government is often counter-productive. - 18, 1126,
1127, 1128
Growth. We have experienced - 683
Guts? Do you have the - 374

H

Habits are best established early in life. - 252
Handicaps. Overcome your - 484, 605
Happened! I'm glad it - 787
Happens. I want to be there when it - 411, 684
Happened. Nothing really - 1269
Happy days are here again! - 6
Happy ending. Either way, a - 241

I

Impossible! It's - 1343
Impressions. Correct wrong - 681, 1333
Improvise! - 116
Incentives. You have - 242, 246
Inconvenient. It's darned - 1028
Incredible! That's - 1117, 1119
Indecision! - 924
Inevitable. The - 113
Inferiority complex. - He/she has an - 1053
Inflation. Fighting - 665, 666, 1260
Influence on fellow human beings. - 147
Innovation is exciting! - 504, 505, 657
Interest! Lost - 125, 855
Interested in a commission? Are you - 50
Invented yet. Not everything has been - 580, 730
Ironical. That's - 495
Irresponsible. We don't need the - 322

J

Jittery. It made me - 21
Job description. - 290, 867
Job for a kid. This is no - 255
Job. On the - 69
Join the club! - 472
Jumping to conclusions. You're - 907
Just in case. - 1240

K

Keep at it! - 156, 731
Kid you not! I - 247, 870, 871, 872, 873
Kindly. Speak - 1102
Kinky crowd. I knew it was a - 1097
Know. More than I cared to - 223
Know. More than you think you - 114, 185, 293, 772
Know. Thought you'd like to - 1412
Know? What do you want to - 364
Knowing things that ain't so. - 152, 234, 969, 1112
Known by their deeds. - 126

L

Labor problems. Don't tell me your - 1153, 1340, 1341
Ladies. A salute to the - 1076
Lately? What have you done for me - 193
Law and order. - 794
Lead. You're in the - 74
Leadership! - 807
Lean a little this way. I - 773
Learner. I was a slow - 1186, 1189
Learning. Always keep - 289, 917
Lesson learned! - 416, 455, 515
Lie. That's a big fat - 1080
Life left in the good old boy. There's - 866
Life isn't all roses! - 492
Life isn't what it used to be - 566
Life that must be. What a - 1283
Logical. That's - 151, 374, 424, 425, 432, 560, 595,
597, 598, 1243, 1251, 1252
Long-winded. Don't be so - 570
Look at it. It's all the way you - 1011, 1300, 1311
Look at. Not much to - 261
Looking up. Things are - 694
Lose! You can't - 131
Lose it all. You'll - 1292
Loser. No one loves a - 922, 923, 1157
Losing. Don't enjoy - 441
Lost, but making good time! - 26
Loyalty! - 738
Luck! Just my - 120, 784, 964
Lucky guy! - 1316

M

Majority rule. - 603
Markets daily. Check the - 582
Marketplace. Remember this about the - 97, 98
Meant. That isn't what I thought you - 1277
Meet him/her on the way down. You may - 957
Memory! Remarkable - 821
Message. He/she didn't get the - 843

Million. Make a - 1398
Mind. Get in a better frame of - 45
Mind your own business! - 1086
Mind. Make up your - 85, 709, 776, 802, 1253
Mind? Are you out of your - 905
Miracle! Nothing short of a - 620
Misfired again! - 251, 516
Mission completed! - 561
Mission. That is our - 248
Miss anything. Don't - 1193
Mistake. It was an honest - 693, 708, 857, 1004, 1005, 1203, 1279, 1297, 1302, 1393
Mistakes. We all make - 55, 146, 214, 224, 281, 283, 296, 297, 370, 554, 612, 697, 1244, 1254, 1352
Mistakes. Learn from your - 951
Mistakes. Don't repeat your - 702
Mistaken idea! - 1027, 1139
Mistaken identity! - 1057
Mixed up. A little - 774
Money. A lot for your - 1025
Money problems. We have - 652
Money. Take the - 1301
Moonlighting! - 295
Moon. Shoot for the - 417, 569
More like it. That's - 711
More like them. How to be - 1165
More than we need to know. That's - 223, 1140
Move, and don't ask questions. - 81
Motivation! - 104, 1034, 1242
Mouth closed. Keep your - 101, 112
Moving! Keep - 615, 1107
Mud. Clear as - 64
Muff it! Don't - 345
Murphy's Law. - 78

N

Need. I always take things I don't - 768
Need it. I don't - 158
Need. That's all you - 782
Needed! You are - 716

Q

R

S

So? Is that - 1261, 1372
Sobering thought. That's a - 865
Sold! He/she's - 346
Sold. Over- - 526
Solution. Simple - 394, 407
Solution. There's always a - 282, 285, 388, 389, 394,
489, 491, 500, 507, 520, 534
Something for nothing! - 688
Spade a spade. Call a - 2, 1370
Speak freely. - 1098
Specific? Could you be more - 749
Speculate. Don't - 1247
Spell it out. With some people you have to - 648, 649,
650
Spend the taxpayers' money. - 167
Spot! On the - 69
Squeal on you! - 5
Squelches! - 1313, 1381
Start? How did it - 331
Stay right in there! - 74, 165
Steady now! - 1281
Steady course. Keep a - 84
Still going on. It's - 148
Stop now. Don't - 159
Straight. Let's get it - 1201
Startling figures appeared. - 1249
Strength in numbers. There is - 900
Struck out. He/she - 133
Stupidity! That's - 32, 68, 546, 600, 1106
Succeed, try, try again. If at first you don't - 447, 521,
593
Success assured - 844, 930, 1275
Success. How-to - 155, 222, 931, 1116, 1118, 1235,
1266, 1276
Success. A little too much of - 94, 519, 932, 1334
Success makes demands! - 100, 599, 1250
Success remembered! - 133, 1041
Success story! - 182, 406, 488, 1180, 1270
Sure? Are you - 728, 845

T

Top us. You can't - 1326
Touched me. You never even - 362
Tough conditions now. So you think we have - 195,
960, 1182
Trouble! So you think you have - 1315
Trouble doesn't even happen. Most of our - 909
Trouble . . . we've got it. - 1, 3, 4, 36, 569
True! True! - 939, 940, 941, 942, 944, 968, 1152, 1198,
1211, 1214, 1215, 1249, 1307, 1365, 1397, 1415
Trust. Misplaced - 301, 910
Truth will come out! - 12, 540
Try again. If at first you don't succeed, try - 442
Try. You can't say he/she didn't - 93
Turn around is fair play. - 1217
Turn? Didn't you know he/she was going to - 240
Turn the wrong way? - 609
Twenty-twenty (20-20) hindsight. - 1266
Two opinions. Always get - 439

U

Understand what we're telling you? Do you - 146,
272, 393, 466
Understanding. Start with a good - 786, 831, 1277
Unnecessary. Dispense with the - 818
Under-statement! - 154
Unusual. A bit - 1088
Up to you! It's - 1280
Use your head! - 1367

V

Valid no longer. - 1363
Version. The revised - 908
Vision. You have to have - 167
Volunteer! - 1166
Vote counts. Every - 213

W

Want? What do you - 307
Warning! Fair - 1092
Watch where you're going. - 37

Y

WORD CROSS REFERENCE

A

Abel 148
Aberdeen, Scotland 1197
Ability 974
Able 1335
Abortion 376
Abscond 282
Absent 1185
Abstract art 61, 62
Abundance 502
Accelerated education 1193
Accent 588
Accept, accepted 265, 276, 370
Accident, accidently 58, 69, 304, 445, 620, 636,
1074, 1157, 1199, 1208, 1240, 1303
Accomplish, accomplished 816, 976
Account, accounts 652, 913
Accountant, accountants 1124, 1290
Accumulates 939
Accused 422, 716
Ace, aces 131, 417
Achieve 11
ACLU 12
Acorns 1236
Acre 393, 486, 496, 1181, 1369
Act, acting, 203, 262
Activist 147
Act of God 1358

Actress 71
Action 727
Actor 1253
Adam 198, 1018, 1138
Add, added 654, 685, 899, 1230, 1244
Address 1180, 1338
Addressed 982
Adequate 1128
Adhesive tape 422
Adjustment 208
Adler, Alfred 971
Administer, administration 56, 391
Admiral 841, 843, 1209
Admire, admirably, admiringly 733, 1058
Admit, admitted 67, 478, 945, 1169, 1325, 1371
Adore 1348
Adult, adults 287, 1283
Adultery 429
Advertise, advertising, advertisement 33, 91, 143,
250, 647, 762, 1009, 1057, 1169, 1337
Advice 166, 439, 498, 651, 717, 1145
Aernonautical 29
Afford 489, 784, 1121, 1247
Afraid 31
Africa 39, 851
After dinner drink 54
Afternoon 54, 1250
Again 6, 403, 790
Against 1056, 1421
Airplane, see Fly
Always 31
Anesthesia 612
Apathy 113
Apfelbaum, Lord Nelson 1209
Apologize, apology 642, 909
Appear, appeared 147, 706, 860, 1143, 1259
Appendicitis 1279
Appendix 1279
Applaud 1082

Apple, apples 187, 198, 327, 490, 825
Application 678
Appraisal, appraisals 1217
Approach, approached 133, 678
Approbation 680
Appropriate 585, 1405
Approve 1261
Aquarium 927
Archery expert 1148
Arena 1094
Argue, argument 132, 173, 391, 596, 755, 830
Ark 934
Arkansas 65, 1238
Arm 64, 620, 918
Army 572, 766
Army Manual 1127
Arrest, arrested 12, 360, 652, 1005, 1188
Arrive, arrival 32, 518, 811
Art 718
Ashtray 669
Aside 1006
Ask, asked, asking 28, 44, 81, 139, 141, 218, 299,
301, 475, 483, 520, 632, 662, 727, 745, 754, 765,
773, 848, 911, 913, 1034, 1038, 1047, 1071, 1094,
1112, 1140, 1148, 1178, 1301, 1336, 1405
Asleep 229
Assault and battery 12
Assemble 604
Assert 192
Assistance 25
Assure 1060, 1128
As usual 1076
At first 1336
Athens, Tennessee 1157
Athens Plow Company 1157
Atlantic City, New Jersey 640
Atomic bomb 1357
Attempt 130, 895, 927
Attended, attendance 189, 242

B

Bad news 210
Baffled 22, 1400
Bag, bags 40, 136
Baggage 1117
Bait 836
Baked Alaska 339
Baker 508
Balance, balances, balancing 211, 507, 1029
Balcony 203
Bald 1202, 1253
Baler 1182
Ball 58, 138, 140, 156, 539, 585, 588, 589, 594
Ballet 64
Ballot, ballots 1006
Ball players 137
Ban 42, 1134
Bananas 327
Band 203, 313
Bank, bank account, banks 209, 488, 652, 1019
Bankrupt 178
Banquet, banquet hall 276, 1076
Baptist 243, 276, 277, 1136
Baptize 243
Bar 45, 249, 418, 430, 435, 436, 446, 1200, 1368
Barbed wire 1375
Barber, barbershop 297, 606, 854, 1242
Bare 300
Bargain 179
Baritone 620
Bark 95
Barkley, Alben 193, 1091
Barn 478, 488, 711
Barnum, P. T. 191, 532
Barracuda 817
Barrel 490
Barrister 1290
Bartender 435, 446, 873, 1281
Base 1122
Baseball 842, 1115, 1122

Believe 151, 352
Believe it or not 827, 1358
Bell 1157
Bellhop 641
Bellyache 687
Belong, belongs 225, 247, 1333
Belt 810
Bend 869
Benefit 148, 203
Beriberi 49
Best 540, 956, 1169, 1210
Best place 1357
Best seller 728, 809
Best way 972
Bet, betting 235, 565, 566, 607, 780
Better 112, 253, 341, 428, 641, 694, 799, 913, 1177,
1274
Better off 1409
Beware 1019
Bewildered 61
Bible 31, 151, 371, 616, 1010, 1128, 1296
Bickering 614
Bicycle 252, 447, 1104
Bid 70, 417
Big, bigger, biggest 34, 96, 112, 152, 526, 547, 597,
691, 753, 1154, 1181, 1326
Big Feather, Chief 651
Bills 6, 7, 116, 161, 376, 399, 719, 847
Billion 902, 1215, 1278
Bingo 206, 830, 1135
Bionic 877
Bird, birds 646, 1236
Birmingham, Alabama 1244
Birth control 117, 1343
Birthday 237, 790, 1029
Bishop 128, 279
Bite 222, 822
Bitter 924
Black 614, 872

Childless 604
Chimney 86, 847, 983
China, Chinese 902, 1380, 1391
China shop 170
Chips 698
Chips are down 948
Chirp up 1076
Choate, Joseph H. 745
Chocolate 1156
Choice 333, 429
Choir 249, 680
Cholesterol 1139
Choose 879
Chop, chopped, chop down 152, 585, 756, 904,
1321
Chords 1389
Chore 490
Christ, Jesus 1197
Christian, Christianity 130, 1141
Christmas 194, 318, 387, 680, 769
Christmas tree 893
Church, parish 131, 243, 247, 279, 781, 1142, 1165,
1217, 1262, 1298
Churchill, Winston 73, 259, 260, 1301
Churn, churned 45, 1109
Cider 1234
Cigarette 456, 669, 838, 851, 1292, 1404
Cigar-smoking 14
Circle 579
Circus 614
Cite 1236
Citizen 601
City 697, 800
City Hall 1350
Civic responsibility 633
Civilized 1368
Civil service 57
Claim 1092, 1303
Clarified 1128

Dallas-Fort Worth, Texas 34, 1325
Damage 1206
Damyankee 1246
Dance, dancer, dancing 64, 517, 1120
Dandelion 713
Dandruff 121
Dare 1421
Dark 2, 15, 555, 1336
Darwin, Charles 631
Dash 451, 1267
Dastardly deed 1016
Data processing center 1413
Date, dates 846, 1196
Daughter 333, 337, 604, 741, 1158, 1182, 1191, 1311
Day, days, daily 10, 186, 236, 316, 317, 389, 446,
503, 556, 573, 582, 626, 692, 702, 733, 842, 896,
938, 968, 1128, 1132, 1155, 1259, 1361, 1366
Days of yore 331
Day off 592
DD (Doctor of Divinity) 278
DDT 648
Dead, see Die
Dead in its tracks 1133
Deadbeat 175
Deadly weapon 12
Deaf 254
Dealer, dealership 528, 1224, 1322, 1337
Dealt, deals 1013, 1041
Dean 290, 296
Dean, Dizzy 135, 1318
Dear 531
Death 1271, 1295
Death benefits 725
Debt 356, 834
DeButts, John D. 1057
Decay 100
Decide, decision 12, 135, 467, 702, 1006, 1261,
1276
Deck 518

Declined 265
Declining rate 1078
Decorum 696
Dedication, dedicated 12, 528
Deed 126
Deemed 1128
Deep 675
Deep South 1006
Deer 571, 643, 1200
Defense 908
Defeat 83, 231
Deficit 209, 692
Define, definition 378, 1141, 1374
Defendent 698, 703, 707
Degeneration 1252
Degrees 1058
Degree, honorary 286
Delaware River 1237
Delay, delayed 32, 852
Delegation 1148
Deliberately 800
Delighted, delightful 680, 892, 1070, 1096, 1363
Deliver, delivery 116, 456, 628, 671, 1338
Demand 1287
Democrat 1007, 1008, 1009, 1010, 1351
Den of iniquity 886
Deny, denies 422, 1040
Deodorant 143, 1278
Depart, departed 909
Dependence 727
Depends 1076
Deposit 859, 1107
Depressed 1202
Depression 1027
Deride, derisively 700, 966
Deserter 1011
Deserve, deserving 804, 1051, 1149, 1178
Desire, desirable 530, 973
Desk 456, 802

Diplomat 1408
Dipstick 861
Direct 1392
Direction, directions 901, 1117
Dirksen, Everett 982, 1215
Dirt roads 1157
Dirty 205, 513, 889, 1355
Dirty habits 205
Dirty look 671
Disagree 319
Disappointment 138
Disarm 908
Discipline 252, 1366
Disco 886
Discouraging 1200
Discover, discovered 276, 441, 467, 588, 732, 862,
911
Discuss 1046
Disease, diseases 332, 620, 730, 820
Disgrace 1028
Disgusted 624
Dishes 764
Disincentives 727
Dismiss, dismissed 12, 919
Disneyland 1359
Disorderly 838
Disorderly house 217
Disorganized 543
Displayed 918
Disposal 322
Disqualify 591
Disregard 903, 1041
Dissatisfied 1148, 1176
Dissertation 1087
Distance 390, 576, 665
Distillery 627
Distinguished 1212
Distribution 1128
Distrust 759

Downstairs 830, 886, 1371
Dozen 706
Drag 79, 1059
Dragged out 755
Drama 548
Draperies 300
Drawback 80
Draw, drawing 64, 1107, 1379
Drawer 1180
Dray wagon 671
Dreadful 161
Dream, dreamer, dreams 971, 1167, 1343, 1411
Dress, dressed, dresses, dressing 368, 442, 755,
764, 1076, 1363, 1383, 1389, 1394
Dresser 620
Dribble 653
Drift, drifting 459, 792
Drilled 1308
Drink, drinking 49, 54, 94, 136, 179, 204, 267, 272,
275, 277, 685, 1233, 1234
Drive, driving, driven, driver, drove 1, 19, 52, 80, 90,
166, 179, 366, 591, 613, 697, 798, 1035, 1127, 1161,
1245, 1389
Drive carefully 17
Driver 59, 1245
Driver's license 355
Drop, dropped 230, 484, 869, 1109, 1116, 1251,
1404
Drops 22, 435
Drought 484
Drugs 176, 819
Druggist, drug store 298, 575, 873
Drunk 1303, 1324
Drunk driver 1292
Dry 245, 484, 1136
Dry eye 12
Duck 339, 414, 1190
Dues 725
Dull 238, 971

Duluth, Minnesota 613
Dumb 177, 648, 671
Dust storms 1326
Duty, duties 259, 1046
Dwarfs 979
Dynamite 1034

E

Ear 1094
Ear-full 797
Early 10, 103, 246, 755, 781, 912
Early bird 963
Ear muffs 445
Earn, earned 576, 701
Ear-rings 695
Earth 150, 691, 1073, 1296, 1415
Earthquake 188
Easterner 1327
Eastern hemisphere 842
East Germany 1162
Easy, easier 96, 252, 316, 567, 571, 1187, 1254
Easy lessons 21
Eat, eating, eaten, eat, ate 276, 373, 383, 388, 636,
784, 909, 923, 927, 935, 1007, 1094, 1169, 1263,
1283
Economic climate 1366
Economic recovery 758
Economic risk 1159
Economic system 1366
Economist 1078
Economy 727, 1125, 1133
Ecumenical 586
Edge 904, 1196
Edison, Thomas Alva 971
Editor 945, 1145
Education 289, 474
Effect 1261
Efficient, efficiency 1024, 1046
Effort 1083

Eggs 152, 234, 496, 1150
Eiffel Tower 64
Eight-hour day 503
Einstein, Albert 971
Eject, ejected 696, 838
Elderly 899
Elders 959
Elect, elected, election 189, 191, 193, 680, 701, 982, 1212
Election board 1006
Election returns 1350
Electric bill 1026
Electric chair 176, 717
Electric fan 1070
Electricity 80, 657
Elephant 1265
Elevator, elevator shaft 45, 53, 222, 1145
Eligible 345
Eliminate 1150
Elude 1276
Embarrass, embarrassment 662, 909, 910
Emerald 695
Emerson, Ralph Waldo 1271
Emotions 371
Empire 833
Employees 919
Empty 77
Empty cab 1213
Enclosed 1149
Encouragement, encouraged 314, 348, 697
Encyclopedia 301
End, ends 111, 260, 411, 458, 507, 508, 545, 892, 1070, 1071, 1076, 1226
Endangered species 708, 1299
Ends meet 735
Enemy, enemies 51, 373, 740, 942
Energy 324, 727
Energy, Department of 172
Enjoy, enjoyment 71, 954, 1394

Evils 1135
Evil thoughts 954
Ewe 37
Exactly 1254
Exalt 966
Examination 537, 538
Examine 402, 1052
Example 919
Exchange 500
Exchange department 1392
Exceeds 1287
Excited, excitement 612, 1180, 1200
Exclaimed 548, 550
Excuses, excused 467, 709
Executed 176
Executive 1148, 1313
Exercise 949
Exertion 1248
Exhaust 580
Expect 242, 291, 676, 790, 925
Expectorate, expectorations 235, 377
Expelled 971
Expensive 397, 473, 595, 1099, 1161, 1406
Experience 469
Expert 106
Explain, explained, explanation 79, 165, 299, 428,
473, 540, 733
Explorer 445
Explode, explosion 46, 485, 850
Export 460
Express train 1118
Extension cord 80
Extra 855, 1193
Extrovert 189
Exult 305
Exxon 436
Eye, eyes 203, 424, 744, 899, 936
Eye-ful 797
Eyelid 470

Eye-opener 54
Eyesight 296

F

Fable 1366
Face, faced, facing 640, 714, 845, 879, 1100, 1175
Fact, facts 124, 969, 1400
Facts of life 475
Faculty 290
Fail, failed, failure 259, 927, 955, 971
Faint, fainted 419, 1112
Fair 415, 489, 567
Fair warning 1092
Faith 257
Fall, fell 203, 422, 496, 733, 1074, 1276
Fall asleep 1092
False confidence 72
False teeth 281, 381, 382, 881
Familiar, familiarity 845, 947
Family 230, 604, 661, 796
Famous 809, 908
Fan 544
Fancy, fancy place 369, 1330
Fan dancer 1083
Far 800
Far apart 482, 801
Fare 30
Far East 851
Fared 913
Farm, farmer, farming 65, 169, 393, 567, 608, 687,
711, 972, 1165, 1177, 1238, 1371
Farm equipment 176, 528
Farm equipment dealer 176, 1182
Far turn 1111
Fashion, fashionable 33, 588
Fast, faster, fast enough 108, 368, 496, 1024, 1104,
1157, 1352
Fat 154, 298

G

Giant 152
Gideon Bible 149
Gift, gifts 510, 769, 1205, 1365
Gimbels 758
Gin 136, 435
Girdle 374
Girl, girls, girl friend 3, 15, 41, 114, 136, 155, 176,
232, 272, 280, 292, 298, 336, 343, 346, 361, 552,
556, 614, 643, 746, 844, 845, 846, 878, 981, 1009,
1048, 1076, 1174, 1210, 1378, 1384, 1400, 1407,
1418, 1420
Give, gave, given, gift, giving, giveth 155, 275, 348,
415, 462, 508, 539, 597, 604, 651, 707, 709, 769,
886, 905, 1099, 1141, 1330
Give up 809, 927, 1109, 1148
Glad 221, 601, 726, 1081
Glands 1131
Glass, glasses 119, 179, 413, 421, 437, 899, 927,
1234
Gleason, Jackie 470
Glided 1235
Glorious 460
Go, goes, going, go out, go after, go back 58, 104,
108, 194, 606, 802, 849, 859, 882, 926, 1017, 1052,
1371, 1379
Goal 377, 379, 390, 571
Goalie 634
Goat 687
Go bananas 687, 1362
God, Lord 30, 86, 172, 242, 250, 255, 271, 280, 303,
373, 415, 462, 502, 680, 712, 720, 743, 1018, 1033,
1034, 1036, 1080, 1262, 1290, 1382, 1418
Goes a long way 171
Goes back to 564
Going to town 1345
Gold 1267
Golf, golf clubs, golf course 267, 1148, 1158, 1170
Gone 451, 859, 1024
Goober 625

Hydrogen 850
Hymn-sing 620

I

IBM 183
Ice 519
Ice box 555
Ice cream, ice cream parlor 1047, 1156, 1283
Ice cube 685
Ice fishing 519
Idea 178, 324, 1024, 1273
Identify, identified, identification 443, 749, 1057
Ignition 569
Ignorant 940
Ignore 272
Ill behaved 225
Illegitimate 279
Ill fitting 346
Illinois 661, 1328
Imagine, imaginative 253, 417, 919, 1411
Immature 943
Immerse 131
Immigration laws 651
Immodesty 540
Immoral 967
Impersonating 652
Immunity 668
Important 529
Impossible 1343
Improve 6
Inactive 1366
Inadequate 127, 654
In between 54
Incentive 242
In charge 807, 1274
Inches 484
Incision 557
Include, included 855, 970
Inconsolable 691
Inconvenient 1028

Italian 192, 555
Item 217
IT&T 1057

J

Jackass 1238
Jack and the beanstalk 152
Jacks 417
Jack up 484
Jail, jailed 12, 217, 501, 702
James, King 1128
Jane 629, 1079
Jars 726
Jeanne d' Arc 555
Jefferson, Thomas 1041, 1129
Jelly 917
Jet 19
Jewelry 695
Jewish 588
Job, jobs 18, 177, 202, 255, 295, 469, 478, 497, 523,
867, 1143, 1210
Job site 1367
Jockey 1111
Join, joining 110, 131, 265, 420, 513, 583, 588, 682,
684, 906, 1238
Joint bank account 1076
Joke 1084
Jones, John Paul 843
Journalist 1143
Joyous 224
Judge 12, 66, 193, 306, 370, 413, 540, 696, 697, 698,
699, 700, 701, 702, 703
July 4th celebration 1084
Jump, jumped, jump off, jumpy 9, 165, 171, 287,
442, 447, 496, 628, 780, 907, 1054, 1116, 1421
Jump at conclusions 949
Jung, Carl Gustav 971
Junior Prom 1076, 1389
Jury duty 709
Justice 700, 978, 1163
Just in case 1240

K

Kangaroo 361

Keats, John 971

Keep, keep off, keeps, keep your head, kept 82, 460, 542, 576, 732, 858, 912, 941, 970, 1037

Kennedy, Teddy 727

Kennel in the sky 1366

Kentucky 193, 616, 625, 661

Kentucky, University of 193

Ketchup 1037

Keyhole 352

Kick, kicked 58, 240, 418, 446, 536, 537, 714, 909, 1101

Kicked out 44

Kidneys 1335

Kids, see Children

Kids (goat) 687

Kill, killed 148, 152, 364, 505, 1157

Kind 1069, 1340

Kinfolks 631

Kings 417

Kinky 1097

Kiss, kisses 273, 764, 778, 845, 984, 1076, 1269, 1283, 1384

Kissinger, Henry 1412

Kitchen 636, 909, 953

Kitty Hawk, North Carolina 1262

Kiwanis Club 263

Knee, knees 33, 514, 889, 1035, 1080

Knife 557, 909

Knit 346

Knock, knock around, knock out, knocker 111, 478, 620, 744, 922

Knot 1231

Know, knowing, known, knowledge, knew 126, 151, 207, 216, 218, 223, 235, 264, 345, 364, 478, 536, 545, 573, 578, 606, 621, 662, 707, 726, 727, 778, 788, 791, 803, 818, 849, 865, 870, 924, 963, 1017, 1073, 1101, 1140, 1143, 1314, 1324, 1356, 1372, 1417, 1420

Know better 1237
Know-how 1177
Knoxville, Tennessee 622
Kovacs, Ernie 1419
Kwai, River 890

L

Label, labeled 528, 840, 1169
Labor 197, 1290
Labor leader 1057
Labor pains 801
Labor problems 1153
Labor union 351
Laboratory 40
Lack, lacks 196, 665, 696
Ladder 476
Ladies first 331
Ladies' rest room 759
Lady, see Woman
Lake 1161
Lame 161
Land 521, 656, 1104
Landed 1074
Landing 23
Landing grounds 259
Landlord 426
Language 546, 831
Lantern 1116, 1118, 1336
Lap 182
Larceny 152
Largest 187
Laryngitis 406, 1156
Last 1110, 1353
Last rites 1110
Late, later 32, 53, 614, 635, 762, 911, 1006, 1026,
1328, 1371
Lather 1129
Latin 206
Laugh, laughed, laughter 247, 459, 601, 700, 1121
Laundry, launder 205, 300

M

Machines 1407
Machine shop 1407
Machinists 1407
Madame 556
Magnetic personality 771
Maiden lady, see Spinster
Mail 1118
Mailbox 300, 447
Mainspring 1076
Main Street 915
Major 58
Majority 603
Make, made 130, 616, 661, 733, 736, 1051
Make a buck 1071
Make a living 40, 736
Make love 530
Make money 1177
Make sure 1239
Make-up 1076
Make up your mind 776
Making good time 26
Malady 22
Male, male sex 273, 732, 815, 1003
Man, men, gentleman 104, 105, 121, 122, 123, 131,
202, 214, 216, 259, 261, 306, 314, 319, 334, 338,
348, 418, 429, 431, 439, 451, 465, 475, 537, 550,
595, 605, 606, 608, 621, 622, 628, 636, 644, 667,
670, 696, 733, 734, 760, 771, 780, 799, 862, 880,
896, 935, 983, 1037, 1075, 1076, 1105, 1118, 1140,
1143, 1247, 1282, 1347, 1371, 1387, 1397, 1398,
1409, 1418
Manage, manages 323, 558
Manager, management 134, 498, 642, 1277
Mandated 1129
Mankind 148
Mane 39

Manhattan 855
Mantle, Mickey 133
Manufacture 182, 216
Marble 124
Marco Polo 839
Marijuana Anonymous 1232
Marines 23, 49
Marker 591
Market 1004, 1136
Marksmanship 1370
Marooned 156, 1371
Marry, marriage, married 56, 158, 176, 198, 234,
261, 273, 346, 351, 353, 394, 442, 604, 630, 637,
671, 673, 681, 894, 1068, 1076, 1260, 1311, 1363,
1398, 1412
Marriage license 1045
Mars 1310
Marshall Field & Company 758
Martini 435, 883
Marx, Chico 1256
Marx, Groucho 265, 1255, 1256
Marx, Karl 1167
Mason 726
Mass 3
Matador 494
Matches 885
Mate 198
Material 1252
Maternity ward 802
Mathematicians 971
Matisse, Henri 63
Matriculate 189
Matter of fact 655
Mattress 13
Mattress factory 46
Mau Mau 513
Maximum 570
Maybe 826, 1016, 1408
Mayflower 659

N

Quarter-pounder 509
Quartette 817
Quebec City, Quebec 1104
Queen 417
Question, questioned, questioner 25, 28, 48, 162,
176, 308, 419, 475, 662, 709, 727, 1077, 1089, 1106,
1252, 1255
Quick, quickest, quickly 44, 203, 276, 608, 1244,
1267
Quicksand 1348
Quick witted 1256
Quiet, quietly 325, 422
Quit, quitter, quitting, quits 175, 221, 439, 442, 462,
497, 523, 616, 1109
Quote, quotes 908, 1127

R

RAF 565
Rabbi 277, 586
Rabbit, jack rabbit 496, 1263
Rabbit out of a hat 1049
Race 74, 79
Race track 709, 937, 1110, 1112
Raccoon 95, 617
Radar 76
Radio 479, 711, 1307
Raffle 964
Railing 433
Railroad, railroad car, railroad crossing, railroad
tracks 419, 433, 478, 503, 780, 1047, 1165, 1336
Rain, raining 102, 123, 484, 911, 934
Raise 480, 565, 662, 895
Raise your hand 1147
Ramp 23
Ran, ran out, run, run over 37, 39, 263, 447, 1157
Ranch, rancher 419, 482
Rangoon, India 54
Rant 1157
Rapidly 1366

Research 819
Reservation 657
Resign 420
Resist, resistance 680, 904, 1224, 1400
Response 1069
Responsible 1265
Rest, rested 165, 1259
Restaurant 330, 357
Rest camp 58
Rest of us 1293
Rest rooms 657, 719, 1369
Restitution 207
Restless 45
Result, results 638, 1129
Retail 831
Retire, retired, retiring 54, 286, 620
Retouch 1410
Retroactive 1343
Return, returned 99, 747, 1178
Revenge 83, 1270
Revenooer 627
Reverse 486
Revise 908
Reward 961, 1158
Rhumba 1352
Rib 1018
Rich, riches 345, 973, 1158, 1160, 1290
Rid, rid of 243, 708
Ride, riding, rode 86, 252, 272, 314, 478, 614, 1104
Ridicule 260, 314
Rifle 843, 1239
Right, rights, informed of rights 12, 298, 326, 703,
906, 1041, 1044, 1303
Right and left 520, 1200
Right direction 1272
Right field 134
Right lane 74
Right out 1003
Right side 32

Rubber 522, 575
Rubber heel 762
Rubber hose 302
Rubbing 1148
Ruined 138
Rule, ruled 460, 522, 975
Rump 65
Run, ran, run into, running, runs 32, 142, 217, 326,
472, 537, 644, 671, 697, 786, 799, 982, 1065, 1116,
1118, 1122, 1236, 1272, 1276, 1333
Run a business 905
Run-down 3, 584
Run loose 239
Running around 695
Running low 74
Run over 909, 1344
Rushing 1279
Russia, Russian 498, 668, 727, 1380
Rut 111
Ruth, Babe 133

S

Saccharin 117, 1134
Sack 47
Sacrifice 1290
Sad tidings 865
Safe 973
Safety deposit box 320
Safety pin 1112
Said and done 931
Sailor 841, 843, 844, 1237
Salary 50, 1293
Sale 1099, 1207, 1211
Sale, for 16
Salesman 156, 366, 432, 677, 678, 1099, 1168, 1169,
1178, 1342
Sales manager 678, 919, 1242
Salesmanship 678
Sales people 1242

Semester 741
Senate, senator 318, 641, 727, 982, 1285
Send, sent 301, 303, 498, 642, 689, 827, 847, 1023,
1117, 1392
Senior play 548
Sentence, sentencing 260, 705, 708, 970, 1128
Sergeant 56, 60, 1238
Serial number 1239
Serious 1206
Serious business 1121
Serious problem 691
Sermon 1262
Serve, served 276, 663, 709, 1042, 1154
Service 24, 244, 274, 531, 609, 641, 1022, 1026
Session 320, 1295
Set 1158
Set 'em up 446
Set the pace 866
Setting 797
Settle 1073
Seven dwarfs 979
Seventh Day Adventist 3
Sew 504, 754
Sex, sex drive, sexes, sexy 505, 870, 898, 1087, 1418
Sexual vigor 826
Shade, shady 1354, 1364
Shake, shaken, shook 255, 601, 1065, 1265
Shaker 435
Shake your head 291, 1177
Shameless 189
Share, sharing 1205
Sharp 1144, 1297
Shape, shaped 156, 1029
Shapely 155, 1076
Shave, shaving 789, 1129, 1186, 1257
Shaving cream 1129
Shaw, George Bernard 73, 971
Sheep 37
Shell 624

Situation 941
Six feet under 24
Six pack 617
Size 103, 596, 810, 923, 1217
Skin 984, 1410
Skip 429
Skirt, skirts 33, 1394
Skull 839
Skunk 562
Skylight 1277
Slack 1191
Slam 224
Slang 235
Slapped 451
Slash 362
Slaves 541
Sleep, slept, sleeping, sleeps 118, 418, 478, 544,
607, 864, 1030, 1092, 1283, 1320, 1371, 1405, 1411
Sledding 195
Sleep 970
Sleeve 131
Slice, slices 109, 276, 588
Slide, slid 143, 182
Slide rule 1389
Slim 135
Slip 203, 490
Slippers 1029
Slippery 182
Slow, slower 461, 650, 971, 1026, 1328
Smacked 419
Small, smaller 152, 547, 548, 557, 691, 1223
Small pox 398
Small town 156, 279
Smart, smarter 97, 177, 194, 327, 457, 571, 671, 930
Smell, smells, smelly 38, 495, 512, 629, 960, 1004,
1278
Smile, smiled, smiling 459, 671, 909, 984, 1109,
1175, 1384, 1411
Smirks 671

Sweater girl 28
Sweat it out 1200
Sweetest 117
Swift 1163
Swim, swimming, swam 16, 252, 484, 1002
Swimming pool 16, 1158, 1249
Swindler 913
Switched 1101
Symptoms 530
Synod 1135
System 510

T

Table, tables 124, 149, 266, 373, 604, 634, 910
Tablecloth 1391
Tablets 117, 774
Tail, tails 756, 1101, 1196
Taillight 89, 615
Tailor 901
Take, taken, took 400, 415, 510, 597, 627, 671, 721,
768, 846, 1004, 1380
Take comfort 124
Taken back 528
Take out 1072
Take your time 789
Talent 706, 1133
Talk, talked, talked back, talking, talkative 70, 268,
607, 624, 658, 705, 723, 873, 892, 919, 940, 1061,
1063, 1073, 1078, 1085, 1135, 1137, 1153, 1243,
1289, 1388
Tall, tallest 256, 1326, 1384
Tampico, Mexico 832
Tanned 1286
Tapioca 317
Target 532
Tarzan 629, 1079
Task 462
Taste, tastes, tasted, tastes good 443, 1151, 1281,
1345
Taut 314

U

Ulcer 928
Umbrella 154, 1190
Umpire 135
Uncalled for 967
Uncle 127
Uncle Sam 1238
Uncombed 456
Unconscious 787
Undecided 1282
Under 13, 842, 889
Underdeveloped 977, 1378
Understand, understood 54, 155, 466, 520, 546, 909, 1409
Understatement 1081
Undertaker 813
Underwear 572, 626, 1240
Undressed 755
Unemployed 202, 211, 596
Unenhampered 1022
Unethical 967
Unfaithful 749
Unfortunate, unfortunately 124, 1041, 1074
Uniforms 33
Unilaterally 908
Uninteresting 155
Union Jack 1104
Unitarian 1140
United Airlines 33
United Mine Workers 351
United States 901, 1056, 1164, 1346
United States Treasury 1261
University 189, 290, 1334
Unknown 151
Unknown Soldier 632
Unlearn 968
Unload 120

V

W

Wag 332
Wage, wages 295, 1343
Wagon, on the 438
Waist 146
Wait, waited, waiting 8, 456, 560, 798, 869, 961,
1002, 1315
Waiter 276, 1152
Wait on you 1219
Waitress 45, 880, 1153
Wake, waken, wake up, woke up 229, 471, 544, 777,
1320, 1324
Walk, walked, walks 171, 456, 574, 575, 618, 629,
667, 700, 748, 800, 856, 915, 948, 981, 1265, 1276,
1348, 1354
Wall 76, 232, 640, 679, 737, 1143
Wall Street 170
Want, wanted, wants, want to 87, 172, 254, 307,
364, 440, 475, 495, 572, 578, 608, 609, 699, 756,
775, 832, 846, 926, 1043, 1130, 1238, 1293, 1364,
1392
Want ad 340, 1009
War 83
War horse 1212
Warehouse 708
Warm 520, 562
Warn, warned, warns 484, 533, 1103
Wash 1129
Washington, D.C. 42, 632, 708, 1131, 1143
Wasp 9
Watch, watched, watchfulness, watching, watch
out 321, 476, 484, 544, 552, 565, 667, 736, 832, 853,
948, 981, 1065, 1143, 1407
Watch dog 1032
Watchman 1336
Water, waters 39, 421, 443, 447, 484, 588, 669,
1129, 1158, 1197, 1319
Waterbed 792

1022, 1050, 1074, 1157, 1162, 1201, 1260, 1263,
1279, 1312, 1379, 1399, 1418
Yearlings 487
Yell, yelled, yelling, yells 500, 593, 667, 983, 1097,
1112, 1122, 1366
Yellow 1190, 1391
Yellow rose of Texas 1324
Yellowstone Park 674
Yes 1408
Yesterday 605, 1080, 1154, 1170
Yield 87, 1317
Young, younger, young folks, young man 734, 790,
886, 887, 888, 899, 904, 929, 943, 959, 1158, 1172
Your Honor 680
Yours 1011, 1200
Yourself, yourselves 11, 745, 777, 951
Youth pills 826, 1005

Zero 36
Zip code 188, 1223
Zipper 45